NEW DIRECTIONS FOR STUDENT SERVICES

Margaret J. Barr, *Texas Christian University*
EDITOR-IN-CHIEF

M. Lee Upcraft, *The Pennsylvania State University*
ASSOCIATE EDITOR

Dealing with Students from Dysfunctional Families

Robert I. Witchel
Indiana University of Pennsylvania

EDITOR

Number 54, Summer 1991

JOSSEY-BASS INC., PUBLISHERS, San Francisco

MAXWELL MACMILLAN INTERNATIONAL PUBLISHING GROUP
New York • Oxford • Singapore • Sydney • Toronto

DEALING WITH STUDENTS FROM DYSFUNCTIONAL FAMILIES
Robert I. Witchel (ed.)
New Directions for Student Services, no. 54
Margaret J. Barr, Editor-in-Chief
M. Lee Upcraft, Associate Editor

Microfilm copies of issues and articles are available in 16mm and 35mm, as well as microfiche in 105mm, through University Microfilms Inc., 300 North Zeeb Road, Ann Arbor, Michigan 48106.

LC 85-644751   ISSN 0164-7970   ISBN 1-55542-798-7

NEW DIRECTIONS FOR STUDENT SERVICES is part of The Jossey-Bass Higher and Adult Education Series and is published quarterly by Jossey-Bass Inc., Publishers (publication number USPS 449-070). Second-class postage paid at San Francisco, California, and at additional mailing offices. Postmaster: Send address changes to Jossey-Bass Inc., Publishers, 350 Sansome Street, San Francisco, California 94104.

EDITORIAL CORRESPONDENCE should be sent to the Editor-in-Chief, Margaret J. Barr, Sadler Hall, Texas Christian University, Fort Worth, Texas 76129.

Cover photograph by Wernher Krutein/PHOTOVAULT © 1990.

Printed on acid-free paper in the United States of America.

CONTENTS

Editor's Notes

During the 1980s, student affairs professionals and others working in higher education became more aware of the number of college students experiencing behavioral and psychological problems and the increase in severity of these difficulties. Such problems as acquaintance rape, bulimia, courtship violence, alcohol abuse, and suicide are almost daily occurrences on college campuses. Requests for prevention programs, and the need for counseling and crisis services to respond to students who have these concerns, have placed further demands on student affairs professionals, especially on staff who work in campus counseling centers and student mental health agencies.

As college campuses encounter these difficult issues, American society is struggling with such critical family problems as divorce, child abuse, incest, alcoholism, and spouse abuse. There has been growing interest in dysfunctional family systems and in adults who grew up in such systems. Professional publications and self-help books have focused on adult survivors of dysfunctional families and have suggested various healing and recovery strategies. Several questions need to be raised among higher education professionals. Is there a connection between the stressful conditions experienced by American families and the perceived rise in serious difficulties among college students? Do college students from dysfunctional families face greater challenges in adjusting to college life? Do campuses have an obligation to provide counseling and intervention services that respond to the needs of these students?

This volume explores these issues and critically examines a number of types of dysfunctional families and their impacts on college students aged eighteen to twenty-two. The volume does not focus on older students who may have grown up in dysfunctional families, since their needs, developmental tasks, and life experiences are different from those of younger students, who are leaving their families for the first time. In the first chapter, Robert I. Witchel presents an introduction to the characteristics of healthy and dysfunctional families alike. Families serve as role models for children and adolescents, and when students enter college, they carry with them emotional strengths and weaknesses from home. Witchel presents evidence for an increase in psychological disturbance among college students. He also makes a connection between growing up in a troubled family and such contemporary student problems as coercive sex, alcohol abuse, courtship violence, suicide, and eating disorders.

Chapters Two through Six explore the most common dysfunctional or impaired family systems and identify major effects on college students. Each chapter also includes suggested programs and services for campuses to respond more effectively to these students. In Chapter Two, Frederick G.

Lopez offers a summary and critique of the available research examining the impact of parental divorce on college students. The special challenges facing many students from divorced families are discussed, and recommendations are offered to assist these students effectively. Chapter Three focuses on alcoholic families and identifies the possible effects of parental alcoholism on college students. Kelly Heryla and Shirley Haberman suggest strategies for assessment and intervention, and they describe models for individual counseling and support groups designed to respond to the needs of college students who are adult children of alcoholics.

In Chapter Four, Linda P. Rouse examines the prevalence of spouse abuse and courtship violence with reference to studies of college students. Exposure to violence between parents during childhood is connected to later involvement in abusive adult relationships. A series of case studies, exploring the impacts of witnessing parental violence, includes material on how college students' adjustment is adversely affected. Chapter Five provides an overview of child sexual abuse and identifies the prevalence among college students of survivors of sexual abuse. Robert I. Witchel reviews the results of a survey of college students, which examined the impact of childhood sexual abuse on students' perceptions of their own current life functioning. Case studies illustrate the critical issues faced by survivors of sexual abuse, and suggestions are offered for staff training, educational programs, intervention strategies, and counseling services.

In Chapter Six, Donelda A. Cook discusses various forms of emotional neglect and their consequences, which often extend through the college years and beyond. Case studies illustrate the visible and not so visible signs of emotional neglect, to assist higher education professionals in identifying students who may be silently crying out for help. As in the preceding chapters, recommendations for programs and services are offered for campuses to respond more effectively to this student population.

In Chapter Seven, Fred B. Newton, a counseling center director, and Robert S. Krause, a university vice-president, offer their observations of the material presented in the preceding chapters and address issues that confront practitioners and administrators. Newton and Krause suggest that institutions assess existing campus and community resources as they respond to the students described throughout this volume. Legal and ethical considerations are examined, characteristic symptoms of students from dysfunctional families are categorized, and a continuum of campus interventions is presented. In the Conclusion, Robert I. Witchel offers a summary and provides a list of additional sources.

In addition to thanking the contributors to this volume, the editor would like to thank his wife, Deborah, for her support, and his children for understanding the time spent working at the computer instead of being with them. Thanks are also due to Barb Townley, Don Woodworth, and Laura

Marshak, for reading drafts and offering feedback; to Berry Barta, who added secretarial support to an already busy schedule; and to Mary Talberg and Stacia Scarletta, for their assistance.

Robert I. Witchel
Editor

Robert I. Witchel is chair of the Department of Counselor Education at Indiana University of Pennsylvania. As a former counseling center director on two campuses, Dr. Witchel has worked extensively with high-risk college students from dysfunctional families. As a licensed psychologist, he has provided therapy to families experiencing difficulties with divorce and child custody, child abuse, incest, alcohol abuse, and other forms of family dysfunction.

*While American families experience significant problems, higher
education professionals are becoming more aware of increases in
psychologically disturbed students.*

The Impact of Dysfunctional Families
on College Students' Development

Robert I. Witchel

Child abuse, divorce, family alcohol and other drug problems, spouse abuse,
and other forms of family violence receive daily coverage in the media:
"Every year close to 2,000,000 children, 2,000,000 wives, and 2,000,000
husbands (yes, husbands) are punched, kicked, beaten up, or injured with
a gun or knife by a member of their families" (Bassis, Gelles, and Levine,
1984, p. 404). Pittman (1987, p. 283) states, "Sixteen percent of couples
have experienced some form of marital violence in the past year. Fifty
percent of high school seniors are hit by their parents, 8 percent of them
actually injured." Every year over a million children suffer from physical,
sexual, and emotional maltreatment (Besharov, 1990), and every other
household experiences some form of family violence at least once a year
(Straus, Gelles, and Steinmetz, 1980). Divorce rates increased sharply during the 1970s, and current estimates predict that one in two recent marriages will end in divorce (Wallerstein and Blakeslee, 1989).

   While the American family is encountering such stressful conditions,
college campuses are becoming more aware of the number of students experiencing problems related to coercive sex, courtship violence, suicide
attempts, eating disorders, and alcohol and other drug abuse. The growing
numbers of psychologically impaired students have placed demands on college counseling and mental health services. McKinley and Dworkin (1989,
p. 31) estimate that "10 to 20 percent of enrolled college students experience enough emotional distress to warrant some type of psychological treatment." Effectively responding to the needs of these students adds to the
challenges facing student affairs and higher education professionals. These

dynamics emphasize the need to critically examine dysfunctional or impaired families and their impacts on college students.

This chapter serves as an introduction to this sourcebook by discussing the importance of the family, including the characteristics of healthy and dysfunctional families; the types of dysfunctional families; how growing up in dysfunctional families affects college students; and evidence of increases in psychological disturbance among college students. A connection is also made between contemporary students' concerns (such as date and acquaintance rape, eating disorders, courtship violence, alcohol and other drug abuse, and depression and suicide) and these students' experiences in troubled or dysfunctional families.

The Importance of the Family

Almost everyone, except babies born with serious congenital problems, begins life with the potential to become a healthy, mature adult. Most toddlers are full of life and in touch with their needs, are creative and curious, know how to say no, and find ways to communicate their needs to others in their environment. Something happens to children on their way to adulthood, however, for lively babies too often become bored, unhappy young adults. The family, representing a child's entire reality when he or she is growing up, determines attitudes, feelings about self, and perceptions of others. While some families accept children's feelings and needs as important, others devalue their children.

Forward (1989 p. 175) states, "Healthy families encourage individuality, personal responsibility, and independence." Healthy families care about the needs and feelings of their children and provide a solid foundation for personal development. The children are encouraged to become independent by developing friendships and engaging in outside activities. By contrast, unhealthy families often have secrets—such as alcoholism, abuse, or incest—that they cannot risk disclosing; therefore, out-of-family activities are discouraged, and outsiders or strangers are not welcomed: "Unhealthy families discourage individual expression. Everyone must conform to the thoughts and actions of the toxic parents" (Forward, 1989, p. 175). Forward (1989, p. 6) also describes "toxic" parents in these words: "Like a chemical toxin, the emotional damage inflicted by these parents spreads throughout a child's being, and as the child grows, so does the pain." Toxic parents often ignore their children's needs, causing emotional or physical pain and damaging the spirit.

Parents in well-functioning families confront problems by open dialogue, identifying and exploring options and seeking support when needed. These parents generally negotiate challenges and resolve traumas effectively. Toxic parents often feel threatened and react irrationally, having little concern for the welfare of their children. These parents are generally unable to cope effectively and resolve stressful situations. Children observe and assimilate both healthy and toxic behaviors exhibited by their parents, who serve as important role models. Teenagers often vow that they will never treat their children the way their parents treated them. Some children growing up in dysfunctional families manage to acquire more healthy life skills and become capable adults and parents. Others, however, adopt such behaviors as drinking and fighting and exhibit poor parenting methods, which remind them of their own parents' actions. Teenagers, including college students who have grown up in violent families, may unconsciously utilize their parents' abusive interaction styles as models for their own intimate relationships. Peele (1989, p. 280) suggests that "those who [develop] insight [are] less likely to repeat the problems they faced as children." A relationship with an emotionally nurturing adult, such as a teacher or a grandparent, can reduce the possibility of repeating dysfunctional family patterns. Experiencing such a relationship during the college years may also have the same positive impact.

In summary, while all families experience conflict and stress, some respond to these challenges in unhealthy ways, including violence toward one another. The family experience, whether positive or negative, often makes a lasting impact on the child and, consequently, the college-age student who is attempting to separate from the home.

Dysfunctional Families

Gannon (1989) identifies five types of dysfunctional families—violent, exploitive, deprived, authoritarian, and addictive—that result in the abuse of children. The types of families identified by Gannon offer a foundation from which to explore the dysfunctional or impaired families described in this volume. A family may take on the qualities or characteristics of one or more of these family types.

Violent Families. In violent families, the most vulnerable members are subject to aggression. The children in such families are often left feeling helpless, for they are unable to cope effectively with the violence. Parents in violent families are often highly punitive, emphasize control, have a low frustration level, and are intolerant of differences. Alcohol and/or drug use often triggers the violence. Gannon (1989, p. 49) states, "In general, violent families seem to alternate between periods of neglect and disengagement followed by periods of violence." These families seem to become most engaged during aggressive episodes, allowing children to connect intimacy with pain, which serves as a model for their own future relationships.

Exploitive Families. Parents in exploitive families perceive their children as personal possessions available to meet their needs (emotional, sexual) or serve as targets of their rage. Children in these families are denied individual rights and needs and often assume household responsibilities (cooking, cleaning) and become primary caretakers of younger siblings. Parents who feel that their needs are not met by their marriage often turn to their children for support; this can lead to incest, the ultimate form of exploitation (Gannon, 1989).

Deprived Families. Parents in deprived families are unable to care fully for their children and often lack emotional and/or financial resources to provide for the family. They typically ignore the children and may leave them on their own for extended periods. The children perceive their parents as uninterested, causing them to feel neglected, unwanted, and unimportant. "At the worst, the parents effectively give up being in charge or taking responsibility for the care of their children. At the best, they provide for the basic needs of their children but neglect them emotionally" (Gannon, 1989, p. 57).

Authoritarian Families. Authoritarian families rigidly adhere to a particular ideology (religious, political, personal), which dominates the purpose and function of the family. "Everything comes second to the goal of supporting the purpose . . . including the child-rearing and the developmental needs of the children" (Gannon, 1989, p. 58). These families often have a rigid hierarchical structure and demand devotion to the authority figure. They use physical punishment, are emotionally abusive, and often prevent the children from engaging in relationships or activities outside the family. The children often feel invalidated and experience conflict when their feelings and desires diverge from the family ideology, resulting in significant uncertainty.

Addictive Families. Addictive families include at least one parent who has an addictive or compulsive behavior (taking drugs, drinking, gambling, promiscuity, spending money, working, eating). "The compulsive behavior is clearly out of control and there is a tendency for the family to organize itself around the parent's addiction and . . . resultant behavior" (Gannon, 1989, p. 62). The children often feel neglected and perceive themselves as taking second place to the addiction. Money is often drained by the parental addiction, leaving limited resources to meet the children's needs. In alcoholic families, the parent is often emotionally and physically abusive while under the influence and, when sober, is often neglectful. The children are blamed, rejected, and criticized, and they internalize the repeated negative messages that will affect them later in life (Gannon, 1989).

While these five types of families represent most of the characteristics of dysfunctional home environments, they are not all-inclusive. Divorced, single-parent, blended, and traditional families can exhibit aspects of one or more of these types of dysfunctional systems, impaired characteristics unique to their situation, or healthy and nurturing qualities. Since the family support system has been identified as a critical aspect of students' making a positive transition to college, it is important to explore the impacts of family dysfunction on college students.

Impacts of Family Dysfunction

The family has been identified as one of the major factors that influence the standards and values of college students. DeCoster and Mable (1981, p. 23) state, "Family members, primarily parents, have provided many years of nurturance and are still viewed by many students as the one stable, reliable source of comfort and counsel." In addition, "there are needs that only parental love and admiration can fulfill. The familiarity, warmth, and memories that are embodied within the family itself contribute to a sense of comfort and security" (p. 40).

The 1980s demonstrated that a significant number of college students come from families that are unlike the nurturing family described by De-Coster and Mable. Many students grow up in family environments that include alcohol abuse, sexual and physical abuse, emotional neglect, violence, divorce, and other unhealthy dynamics. Many of these students have experienced a life based on fear, social isolation, poor communication patterns, inadequate controls and limit setting, blurred boundaries, and abuse of power. These students often perceive the family not as a stable, reliable source of comfort but as a source of pain and confusion. Henton, Hayes, Lamke, and Murphy (1980) found an inverse relationship between availability of family support and perceived adjustment to college. This raises concerns about the ability of students growing up in dysfunctional families to adjust to and be successful in college.

McKinley and Dworkin (1989, p. 34) identify family-of-origin issues as one of four categories characterizing disturbed students: "Many students come to college with unresolved conflicts and difficult personal histories." As some students from dysfunctional homes enter college, they are concerned for the safety or welfare of younger siblings and, perhaps, their parents. These concerns can consume energy needed by the student to effectively separate from the family and adjust to college life and adulthood. Dysfunctional families, as described earlier, have made an impact on their college-bound children, who bring extra emotional baggage to college. According to Hoffman and Weiss (1987 p. 161), "college students can be adversely affected by conflictual relationships within the family, even when they are physically separated from the family while at school." Many adult survivors of dysfunctional families, including college students, experience similar long-term effects, including relationship problems, low self-esteem, self-sabotage (self-destructiveness, attempted suicide, poor choices), sexual problems (inhibition, promiscuity), symptoms of trauma (fear, panic, anxiety, sleep problems, concentration difficulties), physical ailments (eating disorders, headaches, ulcers), social alienation (feeling different, unaccepted, stigmatized), and difficulties in managing feelings.

What follows is a brief introduction to the prevalence of college students who come from the dysfunctional backgrounds explored in this volume, as well as an overview of the effects that dysfunctional families have on students. Throughout this section, increases are reported in the number of students coming from dysfunctional families. It is possible that students have been coming from these kinds of families for many decades, and that the recently perceived increase may not be a new phenomenon. Many adults between the ages of twenty-five and sixty-five, including those who are college graduates, identify themselves as having grown up in dysfunctional families. The recently perceived increase may be a result of counseling professionals' becoming more aware of the issues and of students' being more willing to reveal their backgrounds and to seek services.

Alcoholic Families. Magoon (1989) reports that 189 (85 percent) counseling centers noticed an increase in adult children of alcoholic (ACOA) clients over the past one to two years. In Witchel's (1989) survey of 1,575 college students, more than 17 percent of students indicated that the father, and almost 4 percent indicated the mother, has or had difficulties related to alcohol. Reardon and Markwell (1989), in a survey of college students, found 23 percent to be classified as children of alcoholics (COA's).

Students from alcoholic families, having experienced unstable and confused environments, often struggle with trust as they seek intimacy and relationships. These students are also at risk for problems associated with alcohol and drug use. (Chapter Three thoroughly explores college students who are survivors of alcoholic families.)

Child Sexual Abuse. According to Gallagher (personal communication, 1990), 195 college counseling centers (78.6 percent) reported a definite increase in 1989 in the number of clients reporting sexual abuse as a child. This increase is consistent with rising reports nationally from adults molested as children. In studies of college-student survivors, childhood sexual abuse has been linked to depression and anxiety (Sedney and Brooks, 1984), significantly lower levels of sexual self-esteem (Finkelhor, 1979), and vulnerability to nonconcensual sexual experiences (Fromuth, 1986).

The impact of sexual abuse on a student's early development creates frustrations as the student confronts the developmental challenges of the college years. A survivor may be hampered by a poorly developed identity, feelings of insecurity and isolation, and lack of trust in others. (Chapter Five focuses on college-student survivors of child sexual abuse, including sexual abuse committed by family and nonfamily members.)

Physically and Emotionally Abusive Families. Magoon (1989) reports that 117 (53 percent) counseling centers noticed an increase, over the past one to two years, in the incidence of child abuse–related problems among clients. In a survey of 1,575 college students (Witchel, 1989), 13 percent indicated that they had experienced physical abuse in their families, and 47 percent indicated that emotional or verbal abuse had occurred, with 13 percent indicating that emotional or verbal abuse had occurred often or very often.

In studies of college students, child physical abuse has been tied to courtship violence (Marshall and Rose, 1988) and to thoughts of suicide (Wright, Snodgrass, and Emmons, 1984). Students who, as children, felt unable to please their parents may experience significant stress as they try to meet the academic and social demands of college. (A further exploration of the impacts of emotional neglect on college students is presented in Chapter Six.)

Spouse Abuse. In a survey by Straus, Gelles, and Steinmetz (1980), one out of six couples reported at least one act of marital violence against the spouse each year, and more than one in four couples indicated some type of marital violence during their marriage. In Witchel's (1989) survey of 1,575 college students, 12 percent indicated that spouse abuse had taken place in their families. A connection has been demonstrated between a family background of marital violence, on the one hand, and abuse in dating relationships, on the other (Bernard and Bernard, 1983; Marshall and Rose, 1988; Worth, Matthews, and Coleman, 1990). (Chapter Four discusses the impacts of spousal abuse on college students.)

Divorce. According to Forward (1989, p. 46), "There is no such thing as a happy divorce. Divorce is invariably traumatic for everyone in the family, even though it may well be the healthiest course of action under the circumstances." The purpose of divorce may have been to escape from or dissolve a dysfunctional family; the results, however, may not be what was expected or hoped for. Wallerstein and Blakeslee (1989, p. 303), describe today's families as having more severe reactions to divorce than were observed in the 1970s; they report "more violence, more parental dependence on children, and many more troubled, even suicidal children . . . acute depression in many adolescents . . . a rise in the reports of child abuse and sexual molestation." These effects raise questions about the impacts of divorce on college-age students.

Farber, Primavera, and Felner (1983) questioned eighty-three clinical directors of college mental health centers about reactions of college students to divorcing parents. They saw female students as more likely to seek counseling for the divorce of parents. Numerous problems were seen as statistically more likely for college students facing the divorce of parents, as compared to students from intact families. These included difficulty in concentrating on studies, drug use, sleep problems, eating problems, withdrawal, dependence on roommates, difficulty with intimate relations, depression, anxiety, sexual-identity problems, fears of abandonment, financial difficulties, loyalty conflicts, and feelings of insecurity. It is clear that college students may experience considerable distress over the separation and divorce of their parents. (A comprehensive review of the impacts of parental divorce on college students is presented in Chapter Two.)

Increases in Psychological Disturbance

There has been substantial discussion among student affairs professionals about the perceived increase in psychological disturbance among college students. In addition, models have been recommended for dismissing students who exhibit emotional disturbances (Gehring, 1983; Zirkel and Bargerstock, 1980), as have guidelines for readmitting students after treatment (Gift and Southwick, 1988). The Urban Task Force of the Association of University and College Counseling Center Directors (AUCCCD) conducts an annual study of over 240 urban and nonurban counseling centers. Specific results from these surveys report increases in the number of disturbed students on college campuses. For example, the 1984 survey (Gallagher, 1984, p. 192) of 249 counseling centers indicates that 53 percent "report an increase in severely disturbed students on campus." The 1985 survey reports a similar increase over the previous year (Gallagher, 1985).

Waiting lists in counseling centers appear to have become a sign of the times. The 1989 survey (Gallagher, personal communication, 1990) finds 118 centers (47.8 percent) with waiting lists during busy terms. The 1985 survey reported that 29 percent of counseling centers had problems with waiting lists (Gallagher, 1985). These conditions may indicate an increase in the demand for counseling by more seriously disturbed students. Indicators of serious emotional distress include such self-destructive behaviors as cutting, suicide attempts, and threats against others, as well as psychiatric hospitalizations. The 1987 survey (Gallagher, 1987, p. 54) of 246 centers finds 166 (67 percent) centers that "encountered clients in the past year who inflict[ed] pain on themselves in order to reduce anxiety," and 25 percent of the centers saw that problem as having increased in recent years. Moreover, 79 percent of the centers had been obliged to hospitalize students for psychological reasons (an increase of 15 percent over 1986), 71 percent had had to notify third parties about potentially suicidal students (up 19 percent), and 28 percent had been obliged to warn third parties at risk. The data from these annual surveys support the perception of an increase in serious disturbance among college students and the perception of a rise in behaviors indicative of significant psychological difficulties. These increases in students' disturbance may be real; or perhaps counseling center professionals are now asking more appropriate questions, and distressed students are being more effectively identified by campus staff and paraprofessionals.

Hamilton and Geiger (1984) systematically investigated the patterns of psychopathology among student counseling center clients at Southern Illinois University, in Carbondale. The results of their study revealed that student clients reported symptoms very similar to those of inpatients and outpatients receiving treatment from psychiatric facilities. These findings confirmed the researchers' impression that the counseling center's client population had a significant degree of psychopathology. Further research is needed to clearly identify the factors, such as dysfunctional family backgrounds, that have contributed to increases in psychological difficulties experienced by college students.

Date and Acquaintance Rape. Coercive sex, including date and acquaintance rape, is increasingly recognized as a serious problem on college campuses. College students are considered a high-risk group, since they fall within the age range of the majority of rape victims and offenders; the highest victimization rate for rape is for single females between the ages of sixteen and twenty-four (Koss, 1988). Recent studies on date and acquaintance rape support the prevalence of these behaviors among college students (Aizenman and Kelly, 1988; Miller and Marshall, 1987; Muehlenhard and Linton, 1987; Rivera and Regoli, 1987). Miller and Marshall's (1987) study of 795 college students concluded that 27 percent of women and 15 percent of men reported being forced into sexual intercourse while in a dating situation. Witchel (1989), from a survey of 1,575 students, found 22 percent who indicated that they had been coerced into sexual acts during the previous twelve months.

Many survivors of dysfunctional families experience a sense of powerlessness which makes them more vulnerable to further abusive experiences, such as date and acquaintance rape. Survivors of child sexual abuse are particularly susceptible to incidents of coercive sex (Fromuth, 1986). Students from dysfunctional families often seek the intimacy and nurturance they lacked during childhood, and they also experience considerable difficulty with intimate relationships. These circumstances place them at risk for forced sexual encounters, since they may be misunderstood in their pursuit of intimacy.

Eating Disorders. There has been significant interest during the past ten years in the prevalence of college students who present symptoms of eating disorders. The annual survey conducted by the Urban Task Force of the AUCCCD includes questions about increases in eating disorders. For example, the 1984 survey (Gallagher, 1984) of 249 counseling centers indicates that 40 percent saw an increase in anorexia, while 67 percent reported an increase in cases of bulimia. More recently, the 1989 survey found 14.6 percent of centers seeing more cases of anorexia (up 2.6 percent from 1988), while 36 percent saw an increase in bulimia (up 15 percent from 1988) (Gallagher, personal communication, 1990). Witchel (1989), in a survey of 1,575 students, found almost 25 percent who had experienced symptoms related to eating disorders during the previous twelve months, and 7 percent of the students had experienced such symptoms often or very often.

According to Sargent (1986, p. 2), "Patterns of interaction among families with eating-disordered individuals have been described at length by family therapists. . . . Families with eating-disordered individuals are tense, concerned and highly vulnerable." Krueger and Bornstein (1987, p. 1106) suggest that "roles and communication for bulimic families are significantly more dysfunctional than for normals." The parents often feel insecure, frustrated, and unhappy. The children learn to rely on achievements to gain a sense of worth in the family, but family relationships are weak and unpredictable, and so the children often remain uncertain of their worth and feel isolated (Sargent, 1986). Friedrich (1990) observes a high rate of victimization, most often physical or sexual abuse, among bulimics. Clearly, family backgrounds contribute to development of the symptoms of eating disorders.

Courtship Violence. Studies of high school and college students conducted during the past ten years have reported rates of violence in dating relationships ranging from 12 percent to 65 percent (Sugarman and Hotaling, 1989). In a study of 461 college students, Bernard and Bernard (1983, p. 286) state, "Perhaps the most striking aspect . . . is the extent to which students indulge in the same forms of abuse as they experienced or observed in their families of origin." These researchers also present the possibility that "violence among college students may be simply the link in an unbroken chain reaching from the abuse observed or experienced in childhood to spouse abuse in marriage" (p. 286). Parents who use abusive means to resolve conflicts function as role models for their children, and some students replicate their parents' practices in their own attempts to resolve disputes in dating relationships.

Alcohol and Other Drug Abuse. Considerable attention has been given to the abuse of alcohol and other drugs by college students. Campuses have responded by developing prevention, intervention, and counseling services. White (1989) identifies regular drug use by one or more family members and inadequate parenting as factors correlated with adolescents' drug use. Regular alcohol and other drug use by parents sends messages to children about acceptable standards of use and abuse. Adolescent drug abusers often grow up in families that experience frequent conflict, provide insufficient warmth and caring, and have poor communication patterns. It is reasonable to expect that survivors, in response to the multiple effects of growing up in a dysfunctional family, may resort to using alcohol and other drugs as a means of coping with unpleasant feelings and memories. Some survivors use such substances to cope with the sense of powerlessness, low self-esteem, social isolation, impaired social skills, and inability to trust others. This pattern places college students who have grown up in dysfunctional families at risk for problems associated with alcohol and other drugs.

Depression and Suicide. Westefeld and Furr (1987), in a study of suicide and depression among college students, found that 81 percent of the students had experienced depression since beginning college, and 31 percent had thought about committing suicide. Witchel (1989), in a survey of 1,575 college students, found almost 5 percent who had made at least one suicide attempt during the previous twelve months, and 28 percent who had experienced suicidal thoughts during the same period. Over 25 percent of the students also reported having felt depressed often or very often during the previous twelve months. The family histories of presuicidal youth often include significant turmoil, marital discord, alcohol or other drug abuse, and instability. The parents seem unable to create nurturing relationships to promote their children's self-worth and confidence (White, 1989). If depressed and suicidal students have learned from their families to deal individually and alone with their own problems, they are unlikely to have family support to which they can turn, and they may not possess the skills or self-confidence to reach out to others outside the family.

Summary

As American families experience significant problems, higher education professionals are recognizing increases in psychologically disturbed students, and counseling centers' waiting lists reflect these increases. Families, whether healthy or dysfunctional, provide role models for children, who, when they enter college, carry with them emotional strengths and weaknesses from home. Increased occurrences of coercive sex, attempted suicide, courtship violence, alcohol and other drug abuse, and eating disorders may stem from dysfunctional family backgrounds. The remaining chapters of this volume explore the most common dysfunctional or impaired family systems and identify their major effects on college students between the ages of eighteen and twenty-two.

References

Aizenman, M., and Kelly, G. "The Incidence of Violence and Acquaintance Rape in Dating Relationships Among College Men and Women." *Journal of College Student Development*, 1988, *29*, 305–311.

Bassis, M. S., Gelles, R. J., and Levine, A. *Sociology: An Introduction.* New York: Random House, 1984.

Bernard, M. L., and Bernard, J. L. "Violent Intimacy: The Family as a Model for Love Relationships." *Family Relations*, 1983, *32*, 283–286.

Besharov, D. "Family Violence: Research and Public Policy Issues for the '90s." *Response: To the Victimization of Women and Children*, 1990, *13* (1), 6–7.

DeCoster, D., and Mable, P. (eds.). *Understanding Today's Students.* New Directions for Student Services, no. 16. San Francisco: Jossey-Bass, 1981.

Farber, S. S., Primavera, J., and Felner, R. D. "Older Adolescents and Parental Divorce: Adjustment Problems and Mediators of Coping." *Journal of Divorce*, 1983, *7*, 59–75.

Finkelhor, D. *Sexually Victimized Children.* New York: Free Press, 1979.

Forward, S. *Toxic Parents: Overcoming Their Hurtful Legacy and Reclaiming Your Life.* New York: Bantam Books, 1989.

Friedrich, W. N. *Psychotherapy of Sexually Abused Children and Their Families.* New York: Norton, 1990.

Fromuth, M. E. "The Relationship of Childhood Sexual Abuse with Later Psychological and Sexual Adjustment in a Sample of College Women." *Child Abuse and Neglect*, 1986, *10*, 5–15.

Gallagher, B. "Urban Counseling Center's Special-Interest Group." Paper presented at the annual conference of the Association of University and College Counseling Center Directors, New Orleans, Oct. 1984.

Gallagher, B. "Urban Counseling Center Interest Group." Paper presented at the annual conference of the Association of University and College Counseling Center Directors, Saratoga, N.Y., Oct. 1985.

Gallagher, B. "Urban/Nonurban Counseling Center Survey Highlights." Paper presented to the annual conference of the Association of University and College Counseling Center Directors, Rockport, Maine, Oct. 1987.

Gannon, J. P. Soul Survivors: A New Beginning for Adults Abused as Children. Englewood Cliffs, N.J.: Prentice-Hall, 1989.

Gehring, D. "The Dismissal of Students with Serious Emotional Problems: An Administrative Decision Model." NASPA Journal, 1983, 20 (3), 9-14.

Gift, T., and Southwick, W. "Premature Return to School Following a Psychotic Episode." Journal of American College Health, 1988, 36, 289-292.

Hamilton, K., and Geiger, S. "Clinical Research: Psychopathology in Client Population." Paper presented at the annual conference of the Association of University and College Counseling Center Directors, New Orleans, Oct. 1984.

Henton, J., Hayes, L., Lamke, L., and Murphy, C. "Crisis Reaction of College Freshmen as a Function of Family Support Systems." Personnel and Guidance Journal, 1980, 58, 508-510.

Hoffman, J., and Weiss, B. "Family Problems and Presenting Problems in College Students." Journal of Counseling Psychology, 1987, 2, 157-163.

Koss, M. "Hidden Rape: Sexual Aggression and Victimization in a National Sample of Students in Higher Education." In A. W. Burgess (ed.), Rape and Sexual Assault: A Research Handbook. New York: Garland, 1988.

Krueger, H., and Bornstein, P. "Depression, Sex-Roles, and Family Variables: Comparison of Bulimics, Binge-Eaters, and Normals." Psychological Reports, 1987, 60, 1106.

McKinley, D. L., and Dworkin, D. S. "The Disturbed College Student." In U. Delworth (ed.), Dealing with the Behavioral and Psychological Problems of Students. New Directions for Student Services, no. 45. San Francisco: Jossey-Bass, 1989.

Magoon, T. "The College and University Counseling Centers' 1988-89 Annual Data Bank." Unpublished document, Counseling Center, University of Maryland, 1989.

Marshall, L., and Rose, P. "Family of Origin Violence and Courtship Abuse." Journal of Counseling and Development, 1988, 66, 414-418.

Miller, B., and Marshall, J. "Coercive Sex on the University Campus." Journal of College Student Personnel, 1987, 28 (1), 38-47.

Muehlenhard, C., and Linton, M. "Date Rape and Sexual Aggression in Dating Situations: Incidence and Risk Factors." Journal of Counseling Psychology, 1987, 34, 186-196.

Peele, S. The Diseasing of America: Addiction Treatment Out of Control. Lexington, Mass.: Heath, 1989.

Pittman, F. S., III. Turning Points: Treating Families in Transition and Crisis. New York: Norton, 1987.

Reardon, J. J., and Markwell, B. S. "Self Concept and Drinking Problems of College Students Raised in Alcohol-Abused Homes." Addictive Behaviors, 1989, 14, 225-227.

Rivera, G., and Regoli, R. "Sexual Victimization Experiences of Sorority Women." Sociology and Social Research, 1987, 72, 39-42.

Sargent, J. "Family Therapy Interventions for Anorectics and Bulimics." Family Therapy Today, 1986, 4, 1-8.

Sedney, M. A., and Brooks, B. "Factors Associated with a History of Childhood

Sexual Experience in a Nonclinical Female Population." *Journal of the American Academy of Child Psychiatry,* 1984, *23,* 215-218.

Straus, M. A., Gelles, J., and Steinmetz, S. *Behind Closed Doors: Violence in the American Family.* Garden City, N.Y.: Anchor Press/Doubleday, 1980.

Sugarman, D., and Hotaling, G. "Dating Violence: Prevalence, Context, and Risk Markers." In M. Pirog-Good and J. Stetts (eds.), *Violence and Dating Relationships: Emerging Social Issues.* New York: Praeger, 1989.

Wallerstein, J. S., and Blakeslee, S. *Second Chances: Men, Women, and Children a Decade After Divorce.* New York: Ticknor & Fields, 1989.

Westefeld, J. S., and Furr, S. R. "Suicide and Depression Among College Students." *Professional Psychology: Research and Practice,* 1987, *18,* 119-123.

White, J. L. *The Troubled Adolescent.* Elmsford, N.Y.: Pergamon Press, 1989.

Witchel, R. I. "Child Sexual Abuse and College Students' Life Functioning: Focusing Our Vision." Paper presented at the annual conference of the American College Personnel Association, Washington, D.C., Mar. 1989.

Worth, D., Matthews, P., and Coleman, W. "Sex Role, Group Affiliation, Family Background, and Courtship Violence in College Students." *Journal of College Student Development,* 1990, *31,* 250-254.

Wright, L., Snodgrass, G., and Emmons, J. "Variables Related to the Serious Suicidal Thought Among College Students." *NASPA Journal,* 1984, *22,* 57-64.

Zirkel, P., and Bargerstock, C. "Two Current Legal Concerns in College Student Affairs: Alcohol Consumption and Psychiatric Separation." *Journal of College Student Personnel,* 1980, *21* (3), 252-256.

Robert I. Witchel is chair of the Department of Counselor Education at Indiana University of Pennsylvania. As a former counseling center director on two campuses, Dr. Witchel has worked extensively with high-risk college students from dysfunctional families. As a licensed psychologist, he has provided therapy to families experiencing difficulties with divorce and child custody, child abuse, alcohol abuse, and other forms of family dysfunction.

*Research on the adjustment and development of college students
from divorced families is reviewed and critiqued, and implications
for therapeutic and psychoeducational intervention are discussed.*

The Impact of Parental Divorce on College Students

Frederick G. Lopez

Divorce is a common occurrence in contemporary American society. Half
of all marriages now end in divorce (Peck and Manocherian, 1989), and it
is estimated that, by the year 2000, well over one-half of today's American
children will become stepsons or stepdaughters (Glick, 1989). These sociocultural trends have challenged our traditional conceptions of the family
and have raised important questions about how this stressful life event
(Bloom, Asher, and White, 1978) subsequently affects those individuals
whose lives it has directly touched.

Unfortunately, much of the available research has limited its consideration to the effects of parental divorce on those family members most vulnerable to stress—young children (Hetherington, Cox, and Cox, 1985; Kelly
and Wallerstein, 1976; Wallerstein and Kelly, 1975). Moreover, these investigations have generally focused on children's short-term adjustment and
have failed to consider the possible influence of larger contextual changes,
set into motion by the action of parental divorce, that may also affect longer-
term individual adjustment.

Without question, systematic research on the long-term effects of
parental divorce on children is a difficult undertaking. Given the host of
other background and intervening variables that contemporaneously affect
the course of children's adjustment, isolating the effects unique to parental
divorce would by necessity require longitudinal study of families who are
comparable to one another in virtually all respects except for the experience of divorce. Obvious pragmatic considerations prohibit such statistical
control. Not surprisingly, then, the available literature on the long-term
influences of parental divorce is relatively meager, and findings are fre-

quently inconsistent. Nevertheless, there is evidence suggesting that later life adjustment of the children of divorce is less adequate (Kukla and Weingarten, 1979) and that "parental divorce exerts a lasting negative impact on at least a sizeable minority of the offspring involved" (Kalter, 1987, p. 587). Further efforts to advance understanding of the relation of parental divorce to individual functioning may thus profit from a wide-angle view of this social phenomenon that adequately accounts for the context of affected family members at their different developmental stages and circumstances.

The impact of parental divorce on college students is a specific example deserving of special attention (Lopez, 1987). Beyond facing the expected developmental tasks of consolidating a young-adult identity, forming intimate nonfamilial relationships, and achieving a modicum of psychological independence from one's family of origin, college students are also involved in organizing and implementing long-range educational and career plans and in adapting to the academic, financial, and social demands of a unique learning environment. Does the experience of parental divorce affect students' approach to and resolution of the developmental demands of late adolescence? Do college students from divorced family backgrounds face special adjustment issues that require careful assessment by college counselors and student affairs professionals? What variables may mediate the adjustment of these students during this developmental period?

In an attempt to address these general questions, the present chapter summarizes and critiques the available research examining the impact of parental divorce on college students, discusses some of the special challenges facing many college students from divorced families, and considers how college counselors and student affairs professionals can best assist these students in meeting those challenges successfully.

The Impact of Parental Divorce on College Students: What Do We Know?

The Relation of Parental Divorce to Self-Views, Parent-Child Attachments, and Separation-Individuation Processes. While evidence linking parental divorce with more negative self-views among college students has been mixed (Parish, 1981; Boyd, Nunn, and Parish, 1983), a much more consistent finding in this literature is that students from divorced family backgrounds rate their parents, and especially their fathers, less favorably than do students from intact families (Fine, Moreland, and Schwebel, 1983; Parish and Wigle, 1985; Rozendal, 1983). To what extent do these more negative appraisals of parents affect the course of normal separation-individuation, or the complex developmental process by which late adolescents achieve a sense of psychological independence from their parents? Again, a conclusive answer to this question is difficult.

On the one hand, there is evidence that parental divorce accelerates certain separation-individuation processes during late adolescence and young adulthood (Fry and Addington, 1985), particularly among college-age men who report greater "emotional separation" from parents and earlier "home-leaving" behavior (Moore and Hotch, 1982) and who demonstrate higher scores on measures of ego development, personal control, and identity achievement than do their peers from intact families (Grossman, Shea, and Adams, 1980).

On the other hand, there is evidence that the separation-individuation process among college students from divorced families is not without complication. Lopez, Campbell, and Watkins (1988), for example, found that while both male and female college students from divorced families did indeed report that they were less dependent on their fathers for practical assistance and emotional support, and that they held attitudes and values that were dissimilar to those of their parents, they also reported that they experienced greater conflict, anger, and guilt in their relationships with their fathers than did their counterparts who had not experienced parental divorce. This finding, together with the more negative appraisals of fathers consistently reported by college students from divorced families, indicates that many of these students have not yet achieved a sense of independence from feelings of anger and resentment toward their fathers.

Similar conclusions were drawn in a large-scale survey conducted by White, Brinkerhoff, and Booth (1985). These investigators found that parental divorce substantially weakened the college student's positive emotional attachment only to the noncustodial parent (usually the father); the student's attachment to the custodial parent was generally unaffected. Elsewhere, Drill (1987) presents evidence suggesting that it is not parental divorce per se but rather the reported psychological "loss" of a parent that is significantly correlated with depression among college students.

To be sure, typical conditions in the postdivorce family environment are ripe for such experiences and may pose special threats to the student's relationship with the father (Teyber and Hoffman, 1987). Doherty (1989), for instance, cites national data indicating that 50 percent of the children of divorce have not seen the noncustodial father within the past year, and that only 16 percent see him weekly or more often. In a related vein, Kennedy (1985) found that, relative to their counterparts from intact families, college students from divorced homes viewed their current family environments as significantly less cohesive and more stressful.

Do students who have experienced parental divorce demonstrate greater conflict or ambivalence regarding "home-leaving"? Proulx and Koulack (1987) found no support for this hypothesis; these authors did note, however, that as divorce-related conflict was more openly expressed within these families, students indicated a greater sense of personal control and more positive feelings about leaving home.

Gender-Role Development, Courtship Activity, and Heterosexual Trust. Attempts to explore the relation of parental divorce to students' gender-role development have produced mixed findings and have generally demonstrated that this relation is complex and not well understood. While some investigators have found that college men from divorced homes identify themselves as more masculine and less androgynous than all other groups of their male and female peers (Boyd and Parish, 1984), others have cautioned that observed differences between students from intact and divorced families may be a function of variables that are frequently uncontrolled in this research, such as students' age at the time of their parents' divorce, the presence and sex of siblings, and the presence of postdivorce parental conflict (Vess, Schwebel, and Moreland, 1983). Indeed, while the latter authors found no significant gender-role differences among college students from intact and divorced families, they did observe that males from divorced families exhibiting a high degree of continuing ex-spouse conflict were more likely to describe themselves as having traditional feminine or expressive characteristics. Sexton, Hingst, and Regan (1985) report similar observations; they found that young adult men from divorced families who rated themselves as having predominantly feminine gender-role characteristics also indicated receiving particularly low levels of parental care in their families-of-origin relative to their counterparts from other intact and divorced subgroups.

The relation of parental divorce to courtship activity among college students has produced more consistent findings, indicating that the experience of parental divorce accelerates courtship activity among college students (Hepworth, Ryder, and Dreyer, 1984), especially if there is continuing conflict in the postdivorce family (Booth, Brinkerhoff, and White, 1984). These same investigations reveal that students from divorced families may be more likely to engage in premarital sex and to have a higher frequency of sex partners than will students from intact homes. Students from divorced families have also been shown to have less favorable perceptions of parental childrearing roles (Nunn and Parish, 1982) and to hold more favorable opinions about divorce itself (Rozendal, 1983).

Finally, Southworth and Schwarz (1987) report greater variability in heterosexual trust among college women who have experienced parental divorce, relative to those from intact families. Women in the former group who expressed high heterosexual trust were significantly more likely to rate their divorced fathers as being "accepting" and as expressing consistent love. These rated dimensions of fathers' behavior were also positively correlated with the frequency of postdivorce father-daughter contact.

Adjustment to College. Are students who have experienced parental divorce at greater risk for poorer adjustment to college? Several studies (Adam, Lohrenz, Harper, and Streiner, 1982; Farber, Primavera, and Felner, 1983; Werner and Jones, 1979) have raised concerns about the clinical risk factors associated with parental divorce, but their observations have been entirely based (either directly or indirectly) on samples of college students seeking clinical services. Yet where nonclinical samples of students from intact and nonintact families have been compared on measures of college adjustment, few if any significant between-group differences have been observed (Lopez, Campbell, and Watkins, 1988; Woo, 1981). Once again, there is more evidence that features of the postdivorce family environment, and not divorce itself, explain important variances in students' college adjustment. Flescher (1985), for example, has observed that college students from divorced families where only one biological parent had remarried demonstrated lower adjustment than did students in postdivorce environments where either both parents had remarried or neither had remarried. He has also found the quality of parent-child relations, both currently and at the time of the parents' divorce, to be an important correlate of students' adjustment. In a later report comparing the college adjustment of students from single-parent and stepfather families, Flescher (1986) notes that reported level of extended-family support is positively associated with female students' commitment to college and psychological adjustment but negatively related to the college commitment of male students.

Summary and Methodological Limitations of Current Research

The available research on the impact of parental divorce on college students has yielded only a few consistent findings. First, students from divorced family backgrounds are likely to report negative appraisals of their relationships with their parents, and particularly of the relationship with the father. This may not be surprising, in view of data indicating that only a minority of the children of divorce see their fathers on a regular basis. Second, there is evidence that the experience of parental divorce may accelerate students' progress on a number of developmental tasks, such as achieving greater emotional and functional independence from parents and engaging in courtship activity. Nevertheless, the observation that many students from divorced families harbor lingering anger and resentment toward their fathers suggests that the accelerated separation-individuation process may be less than uniform.

Attempts to link parental divorce with students' gender-role development or college adjustment have not revealed consistent between-group differences but rather have suggested that other features of the postdivorce family environment—such as enduring family conflict or the historical absence of social support—may be more relevant to observed differences on these adjustment dimensions.

There appears little doubt that college students who have experienced parental divorce represent a heterogeneous population, and that efforts to explore group differences by dichotomizing students into "intact" and "non-intact" samples have not been highly informative, particularly when other salient divorce-related factors (level of pre- and postdivorce family conflict, remarriage, and so on) have not been controlled or systematically examined. Given the range of possible postdivorce family environments and their differential implications for relationship quality and stability, it is important that future research utilize designs capable of assessing important process dimensions within different postdivorce family structures. For example, the reviewed research suggests that the quality and frequency of students' postdivorce contact with their fathers may be a process variable worthy of additional study. While some writers have concluded that the father's continued involvement should have a uniformly positive impact on students' postdivorce adjustment (Drill, 1987; Southworth and Schwarz, 1987; Teyber and Hoffman, 1987; White, Brinkerhoff, and Booth, 1985), there is also evidence that the value of frequent father-student contact may vary according to the nature of the postdivorce family structure and the sex of the student (Flescher, 1985, 1986; Lopez and Watkins, in press).

Adjusting to Parental Divorce: Special Challenges Facing College Students from Divorced Families

The available research indicates that the impact of parental divorce on college students is far from uniform and may indeed be the outcome of a complex interaction of students' developmental needs and prevailing conditions in the postdivorce family. Understanding these complex relations requires a metaperspective that views the student as embedded within the larger contexts of both the family and college environments as he or she confronts the normative tasks of late adolescence. The purpose of this section is to consider how the expectable stresses of college may combine and interact with the specific aspects of the divorcing family's adjustment process to create unique challenges to students' adjustment.

The parents' divorce action immediately thrusts the entire family into an unstable period and precipitates the search for an alternative mode of functioning. Hetherington (1982) argues that family systems may require up to three years to restabilize and resume their normal developmental process. This would suggest that students who experience their parents' divorce soon before or during their college years may be especially hard-hit by the demands of an erratic and unpredictable family context. Among the factors affecting the process of restabilization are the family's predivorce experiences and sociocultural context, its economic and financial repercussions, its geographical relocations and visitation conflicts, and its interactional family dynamics after the divorce. Each of these factors will be briefly discussed here, with special emphasis on their relation to college students' adjustment.

Predivorce Experiences and Sociocultural Context. An important background factor affecting the postdivorce adjustment process is the pattern of parental behavior leading up to the divorce decision. For some families, the predivorce period is a long drawn-out affair marked by multiple trial separations, unsuccessful reunions, and personal or marital therapy; for others, the divorce decision is a bolt out of the blue that has been unaccompanied by overt indications of marital stress or unhappiness. Experience indicates that the less expected and protracted the parents' divorce decision, the more disruptive its immediate impact on family functioning, given that less time is available to all affected parties to prepare psychologically for the impending loss.

The level of predivorce marital and family conflict is a relevant background factor. One might expect families to be most favorably positioned for postdivorce adjustment if predivorce family tensions have been high and unremitting and then subsequently relaxed by the divorce action. The adjustment process is probably also moderated by the family's sociocultural context. As Peck and Manocherian (1989) observe, some ethnic and religious groups accept divorce far more readily than others do. Moreover, for some families divorce may be quite common, while in others it is exceedingly rare. These contextual factors may affect both the divorcing family's initial orientation to its altered circumstances and the college student's immediate and subsequent appraisal of the normality of his or her family experience. To the degree that the student's larger (extended) family network is capable of acknowledging, accepting, and accommodating to the parents' divorce decision, that network is likely to remain a viable source of support to the student during this time of stress.

Economic and Financial Repercussions. Crucial to postdivorce family adjustment, particularly for newly single mothers, are financial and economic considerations (Buehler, Hogan, Robinson, and Levy, 1985). Given the demands of college and university tuition and living/travel expenses, these issues are also especially salient to the college student. While specifications for child support accompany all divorce agreements where minor dependents are involved, the bitter reality is that 47 percent of support agreements are not adhered to, and that the incidence of default on support payments has been estimated to be as high as 75 percent (U.S. Bureau of the Census, 1983). Thus the uncertainty of continuing support for college expenses may be a realistic and stress-inducing preoccupation of many students from divorced families, especially students who live with their unremarried mothers.

Related to this concern may be the student's worry for the parent (usually the mother) who is more disadvantaged economically by the divorce. Weitzman (1985) reports that the household income of single-parent mothers declines 73 percent during the first postdivorce year. This precipitate drop often demands that this parent either reenter the work force or significantly increase previous workloads. For ex-wives who have been primarily homemakers in the predivorce family, the sudden demand for workplace reentry can be a jolting, if not overwhelming, experience. A college student in such a family may therefore be inclined to ease the financial and emotional burden on this parent, either by terminating or postponing educational activity or by increasing his or her own involvement in paid work while attending college. Wrestling with these decisions and their immediate and long-term consequences may be another important stressor for the student.

Geographical Changes and Visitation Conflicts. Divorce inevitably entails the physical relocation of one parent. Often this parent or both parents opt to relocate to highly separated areas, making regular student contact with the noncustodial parent (usually the father), and with previous sources of peer and extended-family support, difficult. Nevertheless, a necessary element of postdivorce adjustment is accommodation to new living arrangements and the working out of a satisfactory pattern of contact between the noncustodial parent and his or her children. Visitation arrangements may be fairly prescribed and routine for families containing young children, but by the time children reach late adolescence, parent-student contact patterns may have become quite irregular. This fact may be due to intervening geographical relocations, a remarried parent's greater involvement with a new family or household, the student's increased involvement in peer-related activities, or combinations of these factors. Still, visitation conflicts may reignite during the college years, especially around school breaks and holidays, when students may feel pressured to visit each parent and his and her associated relatives. College students may feel especially ambivalent about visiting a parent who has recently remarried. Visher and Visher (1988) have noted that children in newly remarried families are vulnerable to boundary and identity concerns that are amplified during visitations. Late adolescents, in particular, may experience the pull to join a remarried parent's new family as a threat to establishing greater psychological separation from parents.

Dynamics in the Postdivorce Family. The postdivorce family's ability to address and resolve the financial, logistical, and emotional problems instigated by the divorce action may depend in large part on whether important shifts in family alignment have occurred (or failed to occur) after the divorce. Of principal concern here is the degree to which divorcing parents have resolved or accommodated to the events and tensions that led to marital dissolution. The final divorce decree does not ensure that an appropriate "emotional divorce" has been achieved (Brown, 1989); intense levels of conflict between ex-spouses can persist well into the postdivorce period and become (as suggested by the available research) a better predictor of college students' adjustment than divorce itself.

The persistence of ex-spouse conflict increases the likelihood that the student may be inappropriately enlisted by one or both parents to serve as special confidant, intermediary, or defender in managing this tension. These pressures represent functional demands on the student to remain emotionally overinvolved (enmeshed) within the family system during a time when he or she should instead be assuming a more individuated position within it (Haley, 1980; Minuchin, 1974).

The adequacy of the relationship between ex-spouses may also moderate students' adjustment to the complexity of remarried family environments. Continuing conflict or other unresolved tensions between ex-spouses not only may draw the student into loyalty conflicts but also may threaten the productive engagement of the new stepparent and thus further amplify family stress. These problematic dynamics may be unwittingly exacerbated if the remarried parent or new stepparent is guilty of "overtrying" to achieve happiness and stability in the remarried family (Visher and Visher, 1988).

An important challenge to the college student's adjustment within single-parent families is acceptance of the custodial parent's sexuality and eventual reengagement in romantic relationships. Given that the period of late adolescence already heightens students' awareness of sexuality and intimacy issues, a divorced parent's reinvolvement in dating activities may become a flashpoint of parent-student contention. The clarity of the parent-student boundary regarding dating and sexuality would thus seem to be a crucial organizational feature in the single-parent household. Students who have assumed inappropriate roles in these families, such as parental confidant or parental surrogate to younger children, may experience the entrance of a new adult figure into family life as a threat to their privileged status.

Implications for Counselors and Student Affairs Professionals

The available research suggests that the individual college student who has been negatively affected by his or her parents' divorce may be struggling with any number of issues—intense feelings of guilt, anger, resentment, or abandonment; the loss of social support; worry over a parent's well-being; anxiety over financial repercussions, visitation, or loyalty conflicts; adjustment to the complexity of a remarried family environment. Unfortunately, few campuses offer specialized services for these students (Farber, Primavera, and Felner, 1983). In the hope of stimulating greater awareness of and responsiveness to distressed students from divorced families, key service-related implications of the available research and the foregoing discussion will now be highlighted.

Assessment Considerations

Divorce as Process. College counselors and student affairs professionals must recognize that even the most amicable of parental divorces initiates a disruptive and stressful process requiring multiple adjustments that take time to address and resolve. How well the divorcing family negotiates this transition and ultimately restabilizes into a supportive environment for the college student depends on the family's predivorce structure and climate, its current resources for financial and social support, the quality of the relationship between ex-spouses (particularly their ability to effectively coordinate parenting decisions and activities), and the accessibility of parents to the student.

Service providers should recognize that during the early postdivorce period the family may not be a reliable source of social or financial support for the student, since the parents may be concurrently stressed by their own adjustment requirements. Therefore, attempts to gather information on the family's pre- and postdivorce functioning, financial and social support, and current problem-solving abilities can help establish the level of family disruption precipitated by the divorce and suggest the number and nature of adjustments needed for restabilization. Even in postdivorce families that have been stable for many years, events can occur during the student's college years that may have a destabilizing influence on family and student functioning (for example, a parent's decision to remarry or relocate, the impending birth of a stepsibling, or a change in custodial arrangements).

Family as System. It is also important to recognize that, irrespective of the marital status of parents, the family continues to serve as a significant context for late adolescents' development. Therefore, in assessing students' adjustment difficulties, it may be useful to adopt a systemic perspective that considers the possible interaction of divorce-related experiences and family realignments with students' normal developmental tasks during late adolescence, such as establishing a sense of psychological independence from parents and forming intimate nonfamilial relationships. Research findings that college students from divorced families are significantly more negative in their appraisals of parents (especially fathers) and more likely to report that their postdivorce family environments are more stressful and less cohesive further strengthen this argument.

Students indicating intense conflict with divorced parents are especially at risk for poorer college adjustment. The presence of these family dynamics suggests either that the postdivorce family has not yet stabilized or that it has reorganized into a dysfunctional structure. Careful attention should be paid to the current relationship between the ex-spouses. The presence of continuing conflict in this relationship increases the risk that the student may be drawn into loyalty conflicts and inappropriate cross-generational alliances with one or both parents. Counselors and student affairs professionals should also assess whether the affected student has assumed other inappropriate family roles that may complicate normal separation-individuation, such as serving as a parent surrogate for younger children in the family. The nature and quality of the student's contact with the noncustodial parent and (where relevant) with the stepparent should be carefully assessed as well. Does the student feel inhibited in contacting these individuals directly? Does the intent to make direct contact trigger anxiety for either the student or another family member? Is there evidence that a parent or stepparent may be too involved or "overtrying"? Affirmative answers to these questions may indicate the presence of troublesome family dynamics that may obstruct the student's adjustment and require therapeutic intervention.

Counseling and Student Development Interventions

Family-Based Interventions. Where initial assessments have indicated that disturbed postdivorce family dynamics may be affecting a particular student, college counselors should consider the potential utility of family therapy. The active participation of parents and student would permit a more complete assessment of family dynamics and provide the context for direct intervention. Again, according to the current nature of family organization, the counselor may effectively intervene in a variety of ways—for example, by supporting the development of a cooperative parental alliance, reinforcing appropriate parent-student boundaries, and directly confronting and weakening inappropriate parent-student alliances. Inherent in these therapeutic efforts may be direct instruction in and rehearsal of effective problem-solving skills and assertive communication skills, the dispelling of maladaptive myths (for example, fantasies regarding marital reconciliation and family reunion, expectations of instant happiness in the remarried family), and the encouragement of family members to accept pragmatic constraints and tolerate more permeable family boundaries.

Individual-Based Interventions. Students' maladaptive reactions to parental divorce may be either acute or chronic. With regard to acute adjustment reactions, individual interventions that are short-term, problem-focused, and designed to enhance immediate coping and problem-solving skills may be most effective (Hillard, 1984). Like family-based interventions, such therapeutic efforts may involve identifying and reducing the student's participation in dysfunctional family roles, strengthening his or her communication and conflict-resolution skills, and reinforcing his or her contact with functional sources of peer and family support. The development and regular offering of on-campus divorce-related support groups may help distressed students deal with loss-related themes and benefit from the universality of others' experiences. Huber (1983) describes a cognitively based therapeutic model for helping persons cope with postdivorce emotions, and it could be adapted for these purposes.

The appearance of more chronic divorce-adjustment problems may signal the presence of enduring and highly disturbed family dynamics and object relationships, important delays or disruptions in the student's developmental history, or the complicating influences of affective or thought disturbances, but it may also represent sequelae of significant psychological and/or physical abuse in the student's earlier family experience. These possibilities warrant efforts to establish and maintain supportive therapeutic relationships that promote trust, affective self-disclosure, and the reinforcement of appropriate ego boundaries. Counselors working with these clients may also find it necessary to help students reduce the pressure of academic stressors that may be interfering with therapeutic progress and to coordinate their service with those of other mental health professionals.

Psychoeducational Programming. Increasing the availability of on-campus and residence-hall psychoeducational programming for students and their families may also serve an important function. For instance, during freshman orientation or end-of-the-year family-visit events, presentations and discussions on the importance of positive family dynamics to college students' adjustment may provide a backdrop for special topics of interest to students and parents from divorced families. Topics could include the unique needs and characteristics of single-parent families (Hanson, 1986) and stepfamilies (Skeen, Covi, and Robinson, 1985) or the particular dilemmas facing noncustodial parents (Wilbur and Wilbur, 1988). Such information should raise families' consciousness of adjustment issues and alert students and their families to on-campus and community sources of help. The student affairs professionals responsible for these programs should also be sensitive to how public advertising of these events and programs may effect stepparents' participation.

Conclusion

College students who have experienced their parents' divorce represent a heterogeneous population that is not uniformly distressed by this significant family event. How well the student (and the larger family) adapts to necessary changes precipitated by the divorce probably depends on several factors that, for the most part, have not received sufficient research attention. This chapter has reviewed and critiqued the available research and explored some of the challenges that may face college students from divorced families. Special emphasis has been placed on identifying divorce-related processes that may obstruct or complicate students' development. Counselors and other student affairs professionals working with distressed students from divorced families are encouraged to assess these important process dimensions and to develop therapeutic interventions and programs that will support adaptive family functioning and reduce students' involvement in dysfunctional family roles.

References

Adam, K. S., Lohrenz, J. G., Harper, D., and Streiner, D. "Early Parental Loss and Suicidal Ideation in University Students." *Canadian Journal of Psychiatry,* 1982, 27, 275–281.

Bloom, B. L., Asher, L., and White, S. W. "Marital Disruption as Stressor: A Review and Analysis." *Psychological Bulletin,* 1978, *85,* 867–894.

Booth, A., Brinkerhoff, D. B., and White, L. K. "The Impact of Parental Divorce on Courtship." *Journal of Marriage and the Family,* 1984, *46,* 85–94.

Boyd, D., Nunn, G., and Parish, T. "Effects of Marital Status and Parental Marital Status on Evaluation of Self and Parents." *Journal of Social Psychology,* 1983, *119,* 229–234.

Boyd, D., and Parish, T. "An Investigation of Father Loss and College Students' Androgyny Scores." *Journal of Genetic Psychology,* 1984, *145,* 279–280.

Brown, F. H. "The Post-Divorce Family." In B. Carter and M. McGoldrick (eds.), *The Changing Family Life Cycle.* Newton, Mass.: Allyn & Bacon, 1989.

Buehler, C. A., Hogan, M. J., Robinson, B. E., and Levy, R. "The Parental Divorce Transition: Divorce-Related Stressors and Well-Being." *Journal of Divorce,* 1985, *9,* 61–81.

Doherty, W. J. "New Information on Post-Divorce." *Family Therapy News,* 1989, *20,* 1.

Drill, R. L. "Young Adult Children of Divorced Parents: Depression and the Perception of Loss." *Journal of Divorce,* 1987, *10,* 169–187.

Farber, S. S., Primavera, J., and Felner, R. D. "Older Adolescents and Parental Divorce: Adjustment Problems and Mediators of Coping." *Journal of Divorce,* 1983, *7,* 59–75.

Fine, M., Moreland, J. R., and Schwebel, A. I. "Long-Term Effects of Divorce on Parent-Child Relationships." *Developmental Psychology,* 1983, *19,* 703–713.

Flescher, M. "The Long-Term Effects of Parental Divorce and Remarriage on the Adjustment and Parent-Child Relations of College Students: A Multimethod Study." Unpublished master's thesis, Temple University, 1985.

Flescher, M. "Social Networks and Student Adjustment Following Parental Divorce and Remarriage." Paper presented at the annual meeting of the American Psychological Association, Washington, D.C., Aug. 1986.

Fry, P. S., and Addington, J. "Perceptions of Parent and Child Adjustment in Divorced Families." *Clinical Psychology Review,* 1985, *5,* 141–157.

Glick, P. "Remarried Families, Stepfamilies, and Stepchildren: A Brief Demographic Profile." *Family Relations,* 1989, *38,* 24–27.

Grossman, S. M., Shea, J. A., and Adams, G. R. "Effects of Parental Divorce During Early Childhood on Ego Development and Identity Formation of College Students." *Journal of Divorce,* 1980, *3,* 263–272.

Haley, J. *Leaving Home.* New York: McGraw-Hill, 1980.

Hanson, S.M.H. "Healthy Single-Parent Families." *Family Relations,* 1986, *35,* 125–132.

Hepworth, J., Ryder, R. G., and Dreyer, A. S. "The Effect of Parental Loss on the Formation of Intimate Relationships." *Journal of Marital and Family Therapy,* 1984, *10,* 73–82.

Hetherington, E. M. "Modes of Adaptation to Divorce and Single Parenthood Which Enhance Healthy Family Functioning: Implications for a Preventative Program." Unpublished manuscript, University of Virginia, 1982.

Hetherington, E. M., Cox, M., and Cox, R. "Long-Term Effects of Divorce and Remarriage on the Adjustment of Children." *Journal of the American Academy of Child Psychiatry,* 1985, *24,* 518–530.

Hillard, J. R. "Reactions of College Students to Parental Divorce." *Psychiatric Annals,* 1984, *14,* 663–670.

Huber, C. H. "Feelings of Loss in Response to Divorce: Assessment and Intervention." *Personnel and Guidance Journal,* 1983, *61,* 357–361.

Kalter, N. "Long-Term Effects of Divorce on Children: A Developmental Vulnerability Model." *American Journal of Orthopsychiatry,* 1987, *57,* 587–600.

Kelly, J. B., and Wallerstein, J. S. "The Effects of Parental Divorce: Experiences of the Child in Early Latency." *American Journal of Orthopsychiatry,* 1976, *46,* 20–32.

Kennedy, G. E. "Family Relationships as Perceived by College Students from Single-Parent, Blended, and Intact Families." *Family Perspective,* 1985, *19,* 117–126.

Kukla, R. A., and Weingarten H. "The Long-Term Effects of Parental Divorce in Childhood on Adult Adjustment." *Journal of Social Issues,* 1979, *35,* 50–78.

Lopez, F. G. "The Impact of Parental Divorce on College Student Development." *Journal of Counseling and Development,* 1987, *65,* 484–486.

Lopez, F. G., Campbell, V. L., and Watkins, C. E. "The Relation of Parental Divorce to College Student Development." *Journal of Divorce,* 1988, *12,* 83–98.

Lopez, F. G., and Watkins, C. E. "The Relation of Post-Divorce Family Structure and Frequency of Contact with Father to Parent Adolescent Attachments." *Journal of College Student Development,* in press.

Minuchin, S. *Families and Family Therapy.* Cambridge, Mass.: Harvard University Press, 1974.

Moore, D., and Hotch, D. F. "Parent-Adolescent Separation: The Role of Parental Divorce." *Journal of Youth and Adolescence,* 1982, *11,* 115–119.

Nunn, G. D., and Parish, T. S. "The Impact of Families upon Young Adults' Perceptions of Parental Roles." *Psychology,* 1982, *19,* 7–11.

Parish, T. S. "The Impact of Divorce on the Family." *Adolescence,* 1981, *16,* 557–580.

Parish, T. S., and Wigle, S. E. "A Longitudinal Study of the Impact of Parental Divorce on Adolescents' Evaluations of Self and Parents." *Adolescence,* 1985, *20,* 239–244.

Peck, J. S., and Manocherian, J. R. "Divorce in the Changing Family Life Cycle." In B. Carter and M. McGoldrick (eds.), *The Changing Family Life Cycle.* Newton, Mass.: Allyn & Bacon, 1989.

Proulx, J., and Koulack, D. "The Effect of Parental Divorce on Parent-Adolescent Separation." *Journal of Youth and Adolescence,* 1987, *16,* 473–480.

Rozendal, F. G. "Halos vs. Stigmas: Long-Term Effects of Parent's Death or Divorce on College Students' Concepts of the Family." *Adolescence,* 1983, *18,* 947–955.

Sexton, T. L., Hingst, A. G., and Regan, K. R. "The Effect of Divorce on the Relationship Between Parental Bonding and Sex Role Identification of Adult Males." *Journal of Divorce,* 1985, *9,* 17–31.

Skeen, P., Covi, R. B., and Robinson, B. E. "Stepfamilies: A Review of the Literature with Suggestions for Practitioners." *Journal of Counseling and Development,* 1985, *64,* 121–125.

Southworth, S., and Schwarz, J. C. "Post-Divorce Contact, Relationship with Father, and Heterosexual Trust in Female College Students." *American Journal of Orthopsychiatry,* 1987, *57,* 371–382.

Teyber, E., and Hoffman, C. D. "Missing Fathers." *Psychology Today,* April 1987, pp. 36–39.

U.S. Bureau of the Census. *Marital Statistics and Living Arrangements: March 1982.* Current Population Reports series P-20, no. 80. Washington, D.C.: U.S. Government Printing Office, 1983.

Vess, J. D., Schwebel, A. I., and Moreland, J. "The Effects of Early Parental Divorce on the Sex Role Development of College Students." *Journal of Divorce,* 1983, *7,* 83–95.

Visher, E. B., and Visher, J. S. *Old Loyalties, New Ties: Therapeutic Strategies with Stepfamilies.* New York: Brunner/Mazel, 1988.

Wallerstein, J. S., and Kelly, J. B. "The Effects of Parental Divorce: Experience of the Preschool Child." *Journal of the American Academy of Child Psychiatry,* 1975, *14,* 600–616.

Weitzman, L. J. *The Divorce Revolution.* New York: Free Press, 1985.

Werner, A., and Jones, M. D. "Parent Loss in College Students." *Journal of the American College Health Association*, 1979, 27, 253-256.

White, L. K., Brinkerhoff, D. B., and Booth, A. "The Effect of Marital Disruption of Child's Attachment to Parents." *Journal of Family Issues*, 1985, 6, 5-22.

Wilbur, J. R., and Wilbur, M. "The Noncustodial Parent: Dilemmas and Interventions." *Journal of Counseling and Development*, 1988, 66, 434-437.

Woo, J. "Effects of Parental Divorce on Offspring: A Study of a College Population." *Dissertation Abstracts International*, 1981, 42, 2557B.

Frederick G. Lopez is associate professor of counseling psychology in the Department of Counseling Psychology, Educational Psychology, and Special Education, Michigan State University, East Lansing.

Increased recognition of the Adult Children of Alcoholics' movement by higher education professionals has prompted them to establish programs for college students affected by parental alcoholism.

Student Survivors of Alcoholic Families

Kelly Heryla, Shirley Haberman

The recent demand for institutions of higher education to provide alcohol and other drug prevention programs has stimulated an increase in services directed at students identified as adult children of alcoholics/addicts (ACOAs or ACAs). This increase parallels the heightened societywide interest in the ACOA issue. Anderson and Gadeletto (personal communication, 1989) reveal that services for ACOAs rose from 21 percent in 1979 to 74 percent in 1988.

This increased attention stems in part from the large portion of the population considered to be ACOAs. The Children of Alcoholics Foundation, Inc. (Russell, Henderson, and Blume, 1985), estimates that 22,000,000 people over the age of eighteen can be considered ACOAs. Several surveys conducted on college campuses reveal consistent representation of ACOAs in the student population. For example, Berkowitz and Perkins (1988) found 18 percent of students in their study who indicated that parental drinking was a problem. Witchel (1989) surveyed 1,575 students and found 17 percent who reported that their fathers had difficulties associated with alcohol, and almost 4 percent reported that their mothers had alcohol-related problems. In Claydon's (1987) study of 1,300 college freshmen, 18.9 percent reported parental drinking as a possible problem.

Contrary to popular belief, qualitative differences exist among ACOAs. They do not comprise a homogeneous group, and it is evident that they often experience dissimilar types and degrees of problems (Barnard and Spoentgen, 1986). While it is true that many ACOAs marry alcoholics, it is just as true that others do not. Some ACOAs remain introverted and have difficulty establishing satisfactory relationships, while others mature into adults who develop and maintain fulfilling relationships with spouses, children, and friends. It is critical, then, that those who work with collegiate ACOAs incorporate varying degrees of intervention for ACOA students who seek information and help. This chapter identifies the possible effects of parental alcoholism on college students and their development, reviews the lack of consensus regarding ACOA issues, provides suggestions for campus program strategies, and describes two models for ACOA support groups.

What Are the Effects of Parental Alcoholism?

The primary problem of the alcoholic family is that drinking and drunken behavior become the dominant issues to which family members react. For ACOAs, this means adapting their lives to the unpredictability of the alcoholic's moods and behavior and surviving from one crisis to the next. ACOAs often fail to receive adequate emotional support and attention to their physical needs. In order to cope, ACOAs may develop distorted perceptions of life and assimilate self-destructive behavioral patterns. For many, the result is a decreased sense of self-worth and reduced opportunities to establish productive personal values and goals. In their review of the literature, Van Den Bergh, Hennigan, and Hennigan (1989) note that when ACOAs are compared to non-ACOAs, the ACOAs experience increased rates of physical and sexual abuse, as well as emotional neglect, higher degrees of school-related problems, including substandard academic performance, absenteeism, and suspension; and elevated rates of divorce, violence, and other family conflicts. Understandably, some ACOAs spend a major portion of their time coping with the fear, confusion, and disorganization of the family system. Add to these preoccupations the secretive nature of the alcoholic family, and the outcome is a strong feeling of isolation, along with a disproportionate fear of abandonment, criticism, conflict, and loss of control. Fear often dominates the ACOA's emotional response to life events. The combination of isolation and fear leads to feelings of shame and guilt that result in a reduced sense of self-worth.

At the same time, many ACOAs feel responsibility for stopping parental drinking and preserving the secrecy of the family's problems. Continual failure to accomplish these goals leads to decreased awareness of personal competence. Therefore, ACOAs frequently exhibit an overwhelming need for approval and affirmation, which leads them to change themselves in order to please others. In subsuming their own identities, ACOAs fail to establish or maintain appropriate boundaries for their personal well-being. The outcomes appear to be that ACOAs tend to confuse love with pity, feel mistrust, and are unable to achieve intimacy with others.

Wegscheider-Cruse (1986) delineates four roles that ACOAs adopt in order to maintain balance in the family:

1. The hero, who takes responsibility for and attempts to reduce the family pain by achieving high personal and professional success
2. The scapegoat, who rejects the family system by running away or behaving defiantly
3. The lost child, who attempts to maintain peace by withdrawing from the family
4. The mascot, who covers up pain with humor and attempts to provide comic relief to the family.

ACOAs adopt one of these roles to establish mutually supportive relationships with other family members, which decrease the conflicts caused by parental drinking. In addition, these roles are adopted because both parents frequently neglect to provide children with adequate emotional support and healthy role models. Prolonged exposure to this parental neglect reduces ACOAs' opportunities for personal growth and development of self-enhancing behavior. Therefore, many ACOAs continue to maintain these roles long after they have left their families.

Ackerman (1987a), however, shuns the concept of these mutually exclusive roles, suggesting that clusters of behavior exist and that ACOAs can possess varying degrees of characteristics that cross over several ACOA typologies. He argues that limiting descriptions of ACOAs to a single role may reduce the personal awareness necessary for understanding and coping with their problems. Ackerman emphasizes that the most important aspect of ACOAs is that, although their problems are very similar to those of non-ACOAs, there is a critical difference in the degree to which they experience problems. Thus, college students who are ACOAs may experience problems similar to those of other students but may be less able to discover and initiate productive solutions to the problems they will encounter in the college setting.

For most students college offers a new way of life, where they are expected to master basic developmental tasks. College students are in a transitional stage between adolescence and adulthood and must cope with age-specific developmental tasks. While such tasks as achieving emotional independence, selecting a course of study, planning a career, developing intimate relationships, and achieving autonomy are challenging for most students, they may present an even greater challenge for some ACOAs. Some student ACOAs continue to live at home while they attend college on a full-time or part-time basis. They may continue to be entrenched in a chaotic family, constantly reconciling the differences between life at home and life on campus. Other ACOAs leave home and attempt to move toward a more independent life-style but may find themselves guilt-ridden over abandoning the alcoholic or other vulnerable family members. During holiday and vacation breaks, the student ACOA may experience high anxiety and may try to avoid going home altogether.

Although it seems that some ACOAs suffer from severe emotional, cognitive, and social inadequacies, they do possess skills and talents that should not be overlooked. Many ACOAs have developed strengths that they have simply misapplied. They may have learned to be creative, imaginative, and sensitive to the needs of others as a response to problems within the family. Most would seem to be highly resilient and able to endure hardship and challenges. What is true of ACOAs in general is, naturally, also true of college student ACOAs. While they share many of the same problems of the larger ACOA population, they also share similar strengths.

Parental Alcoholism and Student Development

One effect of parental alcoholism may be that collegiate ACOAs possess a lessened capacity to accomplish the personal developmental tasks expected of college students. The *Student Development Task Inventory* (Winston, Miller, and Prince, 1979) includes three primary tasks that may be particularly affected, and these are described here.

Developing Autonomy. Collegiate ACOAs may have difficulty developing autonomy because of their inability to recognize and successfully attend to their own needs. Their inability to differentiate between their needs and the needs of others blurs the personal boundaries that are critical for establishing independence. A further complication is their tendency to assume responsibility for others. Furthermore, if parental drinking is still active when ACOAs enter college, it may be hard for them to detach themselves from their concerns for the welfare of siblings still living at home, as well as for their parents' safety.

Developing Purpose. Many ACOAs appear to be compulsive and poorly equipped to set limits or define personal goals, They often appear to deal with life in an all-or-nothing manner, alternating periods of irresponsible and overresponsible behavior. This may make it especially difficult for ACOA students to identify career objectives, set academic goals, and develop a balanced life plan that includes work, recreation, and family.

Developing Mature Interpersonal Relationships. ACOAs learn to suppress or deny their feelings, and family rules often prohibit them from expressing feelings. Over time, they learn to distrust their perceptions and feelings, further limiting their range of emotional response and expression. Some ACOA students may be prone to extreme emotional responses to life events; others may appear to be devoid of emotions. ACOAs' tendency to confuse emotions (for example, love with pity) may also cause them to overestimate or underestimate the degree of mutual involvement in personal relationships. Therefore, some collegiate ACOAs may have extreme difficulty with developmental tasks that are generally accepted as normal challenges for college students. Although ACOA students may be extremely competent in meeting some of the challenges of college, they may also suffer from failure in other areas of their personal development.

Research Among College Student ACOAs

Research among college students who have at least one parent suffering from a drug or alcohol problem confirms that some ACOA students possess characteristics and problems different from those of their peers. Such research findings should be interpreted with caution, however. In some cases, studies of collegiate ACOAs have been restricted to clinical populations that are not representative of the entire ACOA college population. In other cases, research findings show few differences, or data that are inconsistent with prevalent beliefs about ACOAs.

In one study, ACOA students were found to be four times as likely to have a drinking problem and three times as likely to have a drug problem as non-ACOAs (Claydon, 1987). A study by Berkowitz and Perkins (1988) reveals that ACOAs are twice as likely to identify themselves as problem drinkers. Rearden and Markwell (1989) found that ACOAs had a significantly lower self-concept than other students did. Daughters of alcoholic and problem-drinking fathers reported more neurotic and acting-out symptoms than daughters of fathers without a drinking problem (Benson and Heller, 1987). Results from another study suggest that ACOAs may be less effective and less assertive as communicators than non-ACOAs (Harriman, 1987). Adolescents with an alcohol-abusing parent tended to report a greater expectation for cognitive and motor enhancement from drinking than did adolescents without a family history of abuse (Brown, Creamer, and Stetson, 1987).

Claydon's (1987) study also illustrates the need to avoid overgeneralizing about ACOAs and the importance of distinguishing between clinical and nonclinical groups. For instance, the ACOAs in Claydon's study were more likely to report a higher degree of self-depreciation than non-ACOAs, yet they shared very similar scores with their non-ACOA peers on seven other personality characteristics, including impulsiveness, independence, autonomy, and the need for social support. Apparently, not all ACOAs respond to their experience in the same way. Some ACOA students may possess constructive survival skills that contribute to their resiliency, and perhaps also a higher than average ability to adapt to life's adversities. Other ACOA students are more likely to lack the emotional and social development necessary to cope with the challenges of campus life. Their adjustment to campus life is more tenuous than that of their non-ACOA peers. Such students tend to share certain characteristics, which suggest that they are poorly equipped to resolve conflicts or adapt to new environments.

The following three cases suggest some of the differences among colege students who participated in a structured support group for ACOAs. Although these three students share the common problem of parental alcoholism, their perceptions and responses to this problem are uniquely different. The first is seriously affected and unable to resolve some of her personal issues. The second has been able to develop a productive lifestyle, despite his father's alcoholism. The third has been able to confront her problems and initiate self-enhancing changes.

Maggie is an ACOA who was also sexually abused periodically by her father, from age four until she left home to attend college. She describes her family as one that did not allow the expression of feelings; signs of affection were rare, and having fun was frowned on.

Maggie has adjusted well to college. She has been academically successful while holding down a full-time job and being a single parent. She appears to be a confident, independent, and happy person. Like other ACOAs, she presents a public image that masks her pain and fear. Her relationships are superficial and guarded. She experiences a great deal of conflict between the person she wants others to see and the person who is still suffering from the trauma of her childhood.

Maggie is most concerned with her inability to maintain satisfying relationships with men. She reports being unable to express feelings easily, is reluctant to demonstrate or receive affection, and cannot accept compliments. She finds it easier to express emotions and intimacy when she has consumed alcohol. Her drinking is neither excessive nor frequent, but the change in her behavior confuses both her and her partners. Although Maggie is aware that these issues undermine her relationships, she firmly believes that she is unable to change.

Maggie struggles with the frustration of feeling unloved and unlovable, yet she rejects compliments and minimizes her personal successes. She wants a relationship, yet she hates herself for being "so dependent and needy." When relationships end, she swings between blaming the man for not accepting her and blaming herself for being unacceptable. She generally feels depressed and overwhelmed with self-doubt. She consistently makes self-deprecating comments, is sarcastic, and maintains belief in her inability to change her behavior.

Although she has more than adequate insight into how her behavior affects her relationships, Maggie believes that "what's done is done" and that it is senseless to "dig up the past." She views intimacy as something threatening and negative, rather than positive. Like other ACOAs, she finds the prospect of changing too frightening, and she has terminated her participation in the group.

John is an ACOA who has been academically successful, has had satisfying personal relationships, and has served as student government president on his campus. Although his father has participated in both residential and outpatient treatment several times, he continues to drink in an alcoholic manner. John is like approximately 75 percent of other ACOAs in that he has not developed problems due to alcohol or other drug use.

John attributes his lack of problems to his involving himself in extracurricular activities and to his determination not to forgo personal satisfaction because of his father's drinking. He believes that even before college his interest in politics and social issues helped him realize that his problems were minor compared to such issues as unemployment, war, and starvation. As a college student, he continued to be a social activist, both locally and abroad. He joined the ACOA group because it was suggested that his "rebellious behavior" was a symptom of unresolved anger with his father.

The group helped John to reaffirm his self-worth and autonomy. Moreover, he provided a positive albeit enviable model to other group members. John has since gone on to complete a master's degree and is currently a doctoral candidate at a major university.

Laurie approached her senior year with anxiety and confusion. She stated that she did not "feel ready to graduate and join the real world." Although she had done well academically, she was not confident that she could assume professional responsibilities and establish full independence from her family and friends. She emphasized that the best thing about college was her membership in a sorority and the ever present support and companionship it provided her.

She revealed to the group that her mother was an alcoholic, and that most of her life had been filled with shame and embarrassment. She described many instances when neighborhood children would tease her because of episodes when her mother's drinking behavior became public. As the oldest child, she assumed many of her mother's responsibilities, including meal preparation, maintenance of the home, and attending to her younger brother. The combination of embarrassment and extra responsibilities kept her from developing friendships and limited her involvement in social activities. Attending college provided a safe and comfortable environment for her, in which she was able to have friends and develop a life of her own. Her life at college helped her improve her self-esteem and identify personal goals that were not supported in her family environment. For Laurie, graduation meant that she had to give up the most worry-free and enjoyable time that she had known in her life.

One of the suggestions made to Laurie was that she attend graduate school. The rationale behind this was that she could further her education and increase her professional marketability while continuing to benefit from her life-style as a college student. Laurie's initial reaction was extremely negative. She felt that she was not "graduate school material" even though she had always been academically successful. Her parents also wanted her to find a job and live at home after completing her bachelor's degree, and she was afraid of letting them down by changing those plans.

Laurie invested herself in discovering what it would require for her to enter and complete graduate school. As she gained more information, she frequently alternated between episodes of extreme confidence and utter self-doubt in her ability to accomplish her goals, and she continued to fear her parents' reaction to her plans.

Disease Versus Development

The dominant theory about ACOAs is that, because they have grown up in an alcoholic family, they suffer from the disease of codependency. Codependency is described as a primary disease, experienced by every member of an alcoholic family, that affects individuals, families, communities, businesses, and perhaps whole societies (Wegscheider-Cruse, 1985; Whitfield, 1989). According to Mendenhall (1989, p. 75), "In spite of our best efforts and some success in putting out the brushfire of addiction, the forest fire [of codependency] is raging and spreading from generation to generation, perpetuating a ripe environment for suffering and addiction."

Peele (1990) explicitly refutes the disease concept and contends that defining commonly shared problems and life experiences as diseases diminishes individuals' confidence in their ability to overcome adversity productively. Marlin (1987) also rejects a pathological view of ACOAs and believes that they should not be burdened with the label of being sick. She points out that all people are influenced by their pasts, and that many non-ACOAs experience the same tensions, anxieties, and fears, even though they did not grow up in an alcoholic family. Her view is shared by Ackerman (1987b, p. 26): "I'm tired of listening to people talk about ACOAs in negative terms only because they possess many positive characteristics, even though these may have been learned painfully." He also expresses concern about overwhelming adult children with an "alcoholized identity" and does not accept that all ACOAs are burdened by dysfunctional behavior or feelings. From his research with approximately one thousand adults, Ackerman describes a variety of ACOA behavior as adult personality characteristics and notes that nine of these characteristics rank as the top ten concerns of both ACOAs and non-ACOAs, suggesting that ACOAs and non-ACOAs share very similar concerns and problems.

Models for Campus Programs

Some ACOAs may spend a lifetime saying and doing whatever it takes to maintain peace and harmony in their relationship with the alcoholic and investing their time and energy in attempting to predict the behavior of the alcoholic, as well as the reactions of other family members. Their strategies may include reducing social involvements, discounting personal goals and ambitions, denying emotions, and distorting reality. How, then, can we best help the ACOA to change? Ackerman (1987a) cites the need for ACOAs to move from this reactive state of living to an active way of life. Cermak (1989, p. 75) states that ACOAs need "time, patience, and discipline" to accomplish long-term productive change.

Recognizing the possible problems faced by college students who are ACOAs, institutions of higher learning are obliged to respond to the perceived needs of these students. Campuses can provide an opportunity for these young adults to break the intergenerational cycle of alcoholism and family dysfunction before their adulthood is firmly established. By providing forums for discovery, discussion, and support, early intervention may enable younger ACOAs to develop better self-esteem and healthier relationships, rather than unknowingly repeating unhealthy relationship patterns learned in the alcoholic family. The following sections outline the components of a comprehensive ACOA program for campuses, including campuswide assessment, individual assessment, awareness and education strategies, assistance and intervention, individual counseling, and group interventions.

Campuswide Assessment. Before implementing programs, campuses need to quantify the ACOA population, qualify the need, and assess existing campus services. Campus assessments should attempt to determine how many students identify themselves as ACOAs, identify the self-reported needs of ACOAs, identify existing campus resources that can provide services to ACOAs, and evaluate the need to implement new programs for the ACOA population. The least intrusive method for gathering these data is to include specific questions designed to identify ACOAs on campuswide alcohol and other drug-use surveys. One or several questions regarding parental drinking and other drug consumption can provide a fairly accurate account of the number of students who may be ACOAs.

More extensive information can be obtained by asking additional questions of those students who acknowledge parental alcohol consumption as a problem. These questions should seek to differentiate between those who consider the effects of parental alcohol consumption a current problem and students who view it as unimportant. An attempt should then be made to identify which students are concerned with personal deficiencies and/ or perceive a need to further develop individual strengths or skills.

Individual Assessment. Campus health care providers and counseling center personnel are in unique positions to intervene with students who are experiencing physical and emotional problems due to parental alcoholism. Campus health care providers frequently see students who demonstrate a high degree of dependency, frequent health complaints, and inadequate follow-through with treatment recommendations. Although these behaviors are most likely shared by non-ACOAs as well, health care providers can identify ACOAs by including several questions regarding parental drinking in the student's health history. Identifying ACOA students not only helps health care providers gain insight into patients' behavior regarding personal health practices but also provides an opportunity to inform ACOA students about available services and make appropriate referrals for further evaluation. An in-depth investigation of parental drinking, personal characteristics, and individual problems associated with ACOAs is probably best conducted by campus counseling center staff.

Counseling center personnel can benefit from screening student clients as possible ACOAs during intake interviews. Identifying clients who are ACOAs may help clarify problems more quickly and assist the clinician with formulating an effective treatment plan.

Jones (1982) had designed the Children of Alcoholics Screening Test (CAST), a thirty-item survey that asks specific questions regarding parental drinking behavior, the individual's reaction to parental drinking, and the emotional consequences. The test specifies the association between parental drinking and problems that may increase the chance that respondents will minimize the severity or deny the existence of complaints. Nevertheless, the CAST appears to have excellent utility for anonymous data collection from ACOAs.

The Adult Personality Characteristics Inventory (in Ackerman, 1987a) attempts to measure the degree to which the respondent engages in specific behaviors typically associated with ACOAs. Using a 5-point Likert Scale (5 = always, 4 = often, 3 = sometimes, 2 = seldom, and 1 = never), it provides a well-defined profile of the respondent's most serious concerns. Because it prioritizes problems, this instrument has excellent utility for developing a treatment plan for ACOAs. Furthermore, this information can be used to match clients' needs with the development of specific goals and objectives for an ACOA group. This strategy can effectively reduce the anxiety and frustration that clients experience when they feel that their time is wasted in a group that does not address their needs.

Awareness and Education Strategies. Student affairs professionals can begin to advocate for the special concerns of ACOAs by increasing the recognition, acceptance, and referral of students. One way this can be accomplished is through public awareness strategies. Outreach flyers and campus bulletin boards are effective methods for disseminating information throughout the campus community. Campus prevention presentations should include guest speakers or films addressing the issues of the alcoholic family. These presentations can identify campus resources available to ACOA students who are interested in learning more about the possible problems of growing up in an alcoholic family.

National Collegiate Alcohol and Drug Awareness Week programs present ideal opportunities for disseminating information and publicizing services for ACOAs. Campus radio or TV channels and student newspapers can be used to advertise schedules of existing off-campus Adult Children's Anonymous or AL-Anon/COA support groups. This strategy not only increases students' awareness but preserves students' freedom to seek or reject participation. It also provides students the opportunity to gain access to information in a manner that maintains anonymity with roommates and friends. Students may be reluctant to pick up printed information, for fear that they will be seen by someone they know or that someone in their residence will see it. Academic courses, such as marriage-and-family classes, psychology and substance-abuse classes, and counseling and social work, offer opportunities for the presentation and discussion of ACOA issues.

At the same time, it is important to consider the lack of agreement regarding codependency and ACOAs. Marlin (1987) suggests the need for a balanced view that considers the strengths and deficiencies of the information and assistance available to ACOAs. Although awareness promotions are motivated by good intentions, staff should consider the possible consequences of information that overgeneralizes or causes inappropriate problem identification and intervention. Extending the message that all ACOAs have a disease that could, without treatment, lead to death may do students more harm than good. Students are more apt to respond to information that stimulates curiosity, expresses a positive message, and instills hope and confidence in ACOAs. Moreover, the setting and the target audience to whom information is disseminated are crucial issues. For example, counseling center personnel find a high number of ACOA students seeking services. There is an obvious need to make brochures, books, films, or audiotapes available, but inserting ACOA brochures into the orientation packages of all incoming freshmen or into mass mailings to all students who live in campus housing, may increase the possibility of inappropriate concern and problem identification. Furthermore, awareness enhancement should be a primary goal, not the means to justify a predetermined goal of establishing broader and more comprehensive services for ACOAs. Therefore, the goal of advocacy should be to provide accurate information that enhances campuswide awareness and response to ACOAs.

Assistance and Intervention. The belief that ACOAs tend to have more problems due to alcohol consumption would suggest that a high proportion of ACOA students may be involved in campus judicial interventions due to alcohol violations. Educational intervention programs for these students are a natural arena in which to disseminate ACOA information. Programs should provide information that describes the biological and environmental factors that increase ACOAs' chances to develop problems associated with alcohol consumption, as well as other dependent or addictive behavior. The program facilitators should also emphasize that students are responsible for modifying their consumption and regulating their behavior if or when they consume.

Facilitators can use this opportunity to identify counseling services and encourage students to seek help if they cannot accomplish these goals.

Individual Counseling. The nearly universal support for the group model as the most effective means for helping ACOAs often overlooks the value of individual counseling, which can be a most effective means of introducing clients to the recovery process. Many ACOAs will not care to disclose certain information, nor should they be expected to, within a group setting. Such issues as sexual preference and experiences of incest, sexual abuse, and other forms of violence may be too uncomfortable for the ACOA to deal with in the presence of other people, even other ACOAs. Some group participants may find that they need more time than a group can offer them. Therapists need to respect a client's right to privacy.

Group Interventions. Support groups for ACOAs are the most widely accepted and popular format for providing help. Groups for ACOAs differ in composition, goals, and members' expectations. The major distinction is between mutual self-help groups facilitated by members and psychoeducational groups led by professional facilitators. Each format has its own distinct advantages and can provide essential help to ACOAs.

The advantage of the group setting is that it provides members with evidence that they are not alone. The group also acts as a source of specific information and education regarding ACOA issues. Moreover, the group offers a safe environment in which ACOAs are able to explore, identify, and express their feelings. Participants can interact with others, without fear of reprisals, judgment, or criticism. The group process can facilitate identification of the survival roles and characteristics adopted by ACOAs that now impair the development of personal efficacy and autonomy. Most important, the different stages of personal growth exhibited by individuals provide group members with alternative choices and role models and can instill confidence for personal change.

Self-Help Groups. Several models for self-help groups exist, and most utilize variations of the twelve-step program originated by Alcoholics Anonymous (AA). One approach for establishing a self-help group, used at the University of Pittsburgh, is the twelve-step model adopted from the Greater Pittsburgh ACOA Network. These steps are taken from Wegscheider-Cruse (1985) and are tailored specifically to ACOAs. The group structure tends to be relaxed and informal, and "cross talk," or open group discussion, is encouraged. Other ACOA groups have adopted a more formal twelve-step program.

ACA groups utilize the twelve steps and traditions adopted from AA. Although the specific format of meetings is not regulated by the ACA World Service Organization, most groups use a fairly standard agenda. Members volunteer to take turns as group leader, opening with a greeting and the Serenity Prayer and introducing a specific topic or theme for the session. The introduction of a specific topic lends structure to group discussions that follow the presentation. Although the discussion most frequently focuses on the leader's topic, members are encouraged to talk freely about any concern or issue.

A significant difference between ACA groups and structured groups is the rule regarding feedback and group discussion. ACA groups enforce the right of each member to speak freely without interruption, questioning, or feedback from other members. This rule is intended to protect ACOAs from criticism, negative attention, or demeaning responses similar to their experiences within their families of origin. Members retain the right to talk, usually for five to ten minutes, or pass when it is their turn. For new members who are not ready to tell their story, this rule minimizes the anxiety and fear of attending first sessions and engenders an atmosphere of comfort. Finally, after every member has been given a turn to speak, the meeting is terminated, and members can take time for informal conversation and socializing. Considering the need for ACOAs to acquire acceptance and affirmation, this may be the most productive function of this group model.

Because there is no charge for these groups, they provide a cost-effective intervention for students and require minimal investment of the institution's financial and human resources. Twelve-step groups do, however, have drawbacks. Wegscheider-Cruse (1989) cautions that some members may take a rigid view of their problems and resist or deny their need for professional help. Criticisms of these groups also include the tendency for some members to continuously review their past and present problems. Such members may become self-absorbed with these problems, remaining stuck in the pain of their losses and never reaching a point of resolution. As in any other group, a time may come when individuals reach a point of diminishing returns regarding the benefits of group membership. This does not have to result in total abandonment of the group but may signal the need and readiness for individual or group counseling.

Some overzealous proponents of twelve-step groups believe that a person accomplishes productive change only through strict adherence to a twelve-step program. Individuals who are not comfortable with the twelve-step approach are often incorrectly viewed as not working through the program because of denial. Many people fulfill their needs through and strongly believe in the twelve-step program, while others have difficulty with the central ideas implicit in the twelve-step model for recovery. Recovery is said to come from the acceptance of one's powerlessness in dealing with problems; one is therefore encouraged to accept a "higher power" as the path to recovery. This concept of powerlessness may be unacceptable to clients who are self-directed and value self-efficacy. Furthermore, the concept of a higher power is most frequently translated into a traditionally Christian viewpoint. Perkins (1987) notes that the college years are commonly the lowest point of religious commitment, and that students' social and academic experiences frequently support critical analysis and sometimes rejection of religious beliefs. Therefore, twelve-step programs may be inappropriate for students who do not accept this orientation in particular or religion in general. When clients' values and beliefs are incompatible with the twelve steps, it is irresponsible and nonproductive to force them to engage in this model. Affiliation with a twelve-step program is supposed to be based on its attractiveness to members, but counselors and other professionals often refer individuals arbitrarily to various self-help programs based on the twelve-step model. They are unwittingly disregarding the fundamental tradition that this is a program of attractiveness. This critical tenet of personal choice must be respected if the program is to continue to benefit those who are attracted to it.

Structured Groups. Facilitator-led groups offer another option for ACOAs to resolve problems and come to terms with the experience of parental drinking. Several models exist for campuses that wish to adopt support groups and other programs for ACOAs. Unlike self-help groups, the structured groups tend to be highly organized and time-limited.

The primary goal of the ACOA group should be to increase participants' self-efficacy—the ability to respond to one's environment in an increasingly self-enhancing manner. Lewis, Dana, and Blevins (1988) emphasize that ACOA groups should stress the development of assertiveness and interpersonal communication skills, along with relaxation and stress-management techniques. Most group formats include education regarding alcoholism and its impact on the communication styles, individual responsibilities, and relationship patterns of family members. A common element of ACOA groups is to have members identify with the roles described by Wegscheider-Cruse (1986). Not all participants, however, can identify exclusively with these roles. Those who facilitate ACOA groups for college students should not rely on dogmatic beliefs to characterize and predict the feelings, perceptions, and behavior of people. It is imperative that facilitators respect the individual differences of students and attempt to find treatments that fit clients, rather than making clients fit the treatments.

The importance of the facilitator's skills and knowledge cannot be overlooked. To be effective, facilitators need to have an in-depth understanding of ACOAs and substance abuse. This is especially true for professionally prepared facilitators who are not ACOAs. Furthermore, facilitators should possess counseling and group-interaction skills, as well as teaching ability. Although personal experience as an ACOA may be beneficial, merely growing up in an alcoholic family is not a sufficient qualification for facilitating a group. Moreover, it is important for facilitators who are ACOAs to have resolved their own personal issues and not to rely on the group to sort them out.

The transient nature of students' participation tends to inhibit the establishment of stable and ongoing group settings. Furthermore, the tendency for ACOAs to avoid commitment, as well as their failure to follow through with responsibilities, requires facilitators to provide cohesion, structure, and direction for group members. Facilitators can avoid problems by developing a clear description of the group's purpose, the time commitment required, and the procedure for students' joining. After a decision is made about who the group members will be, rules and expectations for group members should be mutually agreed on. These expectations should include guidelines for attendance, confidentiality, and interaction of members outside of the group.

It is also helpful for facilitators to know the expectations that members have of the group and to assure members that their needs can be met. Peele and Brodsky (1975) suggest that the focus for improving people's lives should be helping them to realize their ideals, rather than remedy their defects. Considering the lack of consensus on how best to help ACOAs, this may be the most productive approach to take with college ACOAs.

Summary

The challenge to establish effective and appropriate campuswide programs for alcohol and drug prevention is fraught with theoretical, philosophical, and empirical disagreements. Growing up in an alcoholic family can negatively affect the development of some college students. It may be difficult for some ACOA students to respond effectively to the different environment and experiences of college life. Questions exist regarding the types of services to be implemented for ACOAs. Campus personnel should consider the breadth of information, especially the lack of consensus within the literature, in planning and implementing services for ACOAs. To adequately address the needs of these students, assessment, intervention, awareness and education strategies, and individual and group counseling models have been suggested. All campuses should be able to identify at least one service they can offer to ACOA students. Ideally, a campus should choose to offer a comprehensive selection of programs and services to more fully meet the needs of its student body.

References

Ackerman, R. *Let Go and Grow.* Deerfield Beach, Fla.: Health Communications, 1987a.

Ackerman, R. "A New Perspective on Adult Children of Alcoholics." *EAP Digest,* January/February 1987b, pp. 25–29.

Barnard, C., and Spoentgen, P. "Children of Alcoholics: Characteristics and Treatment." *Alcoholism Treatment Quarterly,* 1986, 3, 47–65.

Benson, C. S., and Heller, K. "Factors in the Current Adjustment of Young Adult Daughters of Alcoholic and Problem Drinking Fathers." *Journal of Abnormal Psychology,* 1987, 96 (4), 305–311.

Berkowitz, A., and Perkins, H. W. "Personality Characteristics of Children of Alcoholics." *Journal of Consulting and Clinical Psychology,* 1988, 56 (2), 117–121.

Brown, S., Creamer, V., and Stetson, B. "Adolescent Alcohol Expectancies in Relation to Personal and Parental Drinking Patterns." *Journal of Abnormal Psychology,* 1987, 97 (2), 206–217.

Cermak, T. *A Primer on Adult Children of Alcoholics.* Deerfield Beach, Fla.: Health Communications, 1989.

Claydon, P. "Self-Reported Alcohol, Drug, and Eating Disorder Problems Among Male and Female Collegiate Children of Alcoholics." *Journal of American College Health,* 1987, 36, 111–116.

Harriman, S. G. "Identification and Evaluation of Communicator Style in Adult Children of Alcoholic Parents." Paper presented at the annual meeting of the Western Speech Communication Association, Salt Lake City, Feb. 1987.

Jones, J. *Preliminary Test Manual: The Children of Alcoholics Screening Test.* Chicago: Family Recovery Press, 1982.

Lewis, J., Dana, R., and Blevins, G. *Substance Abuse Counseling: An Individualized Approach.* Monterey, Calif.: Brooks/Cole, 1988.

Marlin, E. *Hope: New Choices and Recovery Strategies for Adult Children of Alcoholics.* New York: Harper & Row, 1987.

Mendenhall, W. "Co-Dependency Definitions and Dynamics." *Alcoholism Treatment Quarterly,* 1989, *6,* 3–17, 75.

Peele, S. "New Jersey Q & A, Addiction and the 'Disease Mythology.' " *New York Times,* Mar. 18, 1990, Sect. 12, p. 3.

Peele, S., and Brodsky, A. *Love and Addiction.* New York: Taplinger Publishing, 1975.

Perkins, H. W. "Parental Religion and Alcohol Use Problems as Intergenerational Predictors of Problem Drinking Among College Youth." *Journal for the Scientific Study of Religion,* 1987, *26,* (3), 340–357.

Rearden, J. J., and Markwell, B. S. "Self Concept and Drinking Problems of College Students Raised in Alcohol-Abused Homes." *Addictive Behaviors,* 1989, *14,* 225–227.

Russell, M., Henderson, C., and Blume, S. *Children of Alcoholics: A Review of the Literature.* New York: Children of Alcoholics Foundation, 1985.

Van Den Bergh, M., Hennigan, K., and Hennigan, D. "Children of Parents in Drug/Alcohol Programs: Are They Underserved?" *Alcoholism Treatment Quarterly,* 1989, *6,* 1–25.

Wegscheider-Cruse, S. *Choicemaking: For Co-Dependents, Adult Children and Spirituality Seekers.* Deerfield Beach, Fla.: Health Communications, 1985.

Wegscheider-Cruse, S. "From Reconstruction to Restoration." In R. J. Ackerman (ed.), *Growing in the Shadow.* Deerfield Beach, Fla.: Health Communications, 1986.

Wegscheider-Cruse, S. *The Miracle of Recovery.* Deerfield Beach, Fla.: Health Communications, 1989.

Whitfield, C. "Co-Dependence: Our Most Common Addiction—Some Physical, Mental, Emotional and Spiritual Perspectives." *Alcoholism Treatment Quarterly,* 1989, *6,* 19–36.

Winston, R., Miller, T., and Prince, J. *The Student Development Task Inventory.* Athens, Ga.: Student Development Associates, 1979.

Witchel, R. I. "Child Sexual Abuse and College Students' Life Functioning: Focusing Our Vision." Paper presented at the annual conference of the American College Personnel Association, Washington, D.C., Mar. 1989.

Kelly Heryla is a certified prevention specialist and coordinator of Chemical Health Awareness and Management Programs (CHAMP) of Indiana University of Pennsylvania (IUP). In 1984, he initiated the IUP Chemical Health Program, and in 1988 he established Project REACH (Realistic Education for Attaining Chemical Health).

Shirley Haberman is health education administrator for the Student Health Service at the University of Pittsburgh, Pennsylvania.

Students' involvement in violence in dating relationships and other interpersonal problems may be a result of earlier exposure to the use of physical force between parents.

College Students and the Legacy of Spouse Abuse

Linda P. Rouse

Students arrive at college with a social history that has shaped the way they think, feel, and behave. One important part of this history is family background. Steinmetz and Straus (1973) suggest a powerful image of the family as a "cradle of violence," a social learning environment. Families do not always conform to the ideal of a consistently supportive and nurturing environment for childrearing. Research on family violence has shown instead that physical abuse is a widespread occurrence in American families. Various types of family violence have been identified, but this chapter focuses specifically on the impact of spouse abuse.

The following section documents the prevalence of spouse abuse and courtship violence, with reference to studies of college students. Next, the relationship between childhood exposure to violence between parents and later involvement in abusive adult relationships is examined. The impact of witnessing violence between parents is explored in later sections, through discussion of a series of individual cases. The first two cases introduce the violent family, as viewed by children of battered women. The next two cases describe children in late adolescence and early adulthood, showing the long-term effects of the spousal violence that led to their parents' divorce. The final three cases illustrate how childhood exposure to spouse abuse may adversely affect college students' adjustment. Psychodynamic and social learning theories are used to frame an understanding of the legacy of violence between parents. In the final section, intervention strategies beyond individual counseling are considered.

NEW DIRECTIONS FOR STUDENT SERVICES, no. 54, Summer 1991 © Jossey-Bass Inc., Publishers

Prevalence of Spouse Abuse and Courtship Violence

Flynn (1977) reports a conservative estimate that at least one incident involving moderate to severe spousal assault takes place in one out of ten families in any given year. At least 1.8 million women are severely battered each year by a man with whom they live (Hotaling, Finkelhor, Kirkpatrick, and Straus, 1988). According to the FBI, that is about one beating every twenty seconds. Studies of divorce applications, such as O'Brien (1971), have also shown that one-fifth or more of women interviewed cite physical abuse as a major complaint. With spousal assault so pervasive in American society, it seems reasonable to assume that many college students have grown up with violence in the home.

College freshmen responding to a questionnaire concerning conflicts that occurred during their high school senior year reported that 16 percent of their parents had used physical force against each other (Steinmetz and Straus, 1973). Since these figures are for a single year, they underestimate the percentage of students who have ever seen force used between parents, and they do not include incidents between parents that went unobserved by the student but may have contributed to a dysfunctional family climate. The types of parental behavior considered included hitting, pushing, kicking, and throwing things at one another in the course of a quarrel. These behaviors were regarded as "conflict tactics" (Straus, 1979), placing spousal assault in the social context of strategies for responding to conflict. As students are growing up, parents provide an important model for how conflicts should be handled in interpersonal relationships. Realistically, conflicts among family members are inevitable. Children may learn constructive, positive methods for resolving such conflicts or may observe that physical force is used in these encounters, as a result of anger (expressive violence) or to obtain compliance (instrumental violence).

Makepeace (1981) found that one-fifth of the 202 college students responding to his questionnaire had themselves experienced some type of courtship violence. Similarly, Rouse, Breen, and Howell (1988) found that 28.2 percent of their sample of 585 never-married students, heterosexual and dating, had been pushed, grabbed, or shoved by a dating partner, that 17.4 percent had been struck, slapped, or punched, and that 11 percent had suffered the consequences, such as visible injuries and medical or police intervention, of more severe abuse.

Intergenerational Transmission of Violence

In keeping with social learning theory, we would expect college students who are using physical force in their own marital or dating relationships to be more likely than other college students to report use of physical force between parents in their families of origin. The "intergenerational transmission of violence" hypothesis is consistent with the picture that emerged from Bernard and Bernard's (1983) survey of 461 college students. Eighty-eight (19 percent) of these students reported that they had been physically abusive in a dating relationship. Although not all students from abusive family backgrounds will display abusive behavior toward a dating partner, students in this sample were found more likely to be abusive if they had experienced or observed abuse in their family of origin.

Altogether, 50 (34 percent) of the 149 students reporting an abusive family background had themselves engaged in physical violence toward a dating partner, as compared to 38 (12 percent) of the 312 students reporting a nonabusive family background. Moreover, for both men and women, about three-fourths of those who had observed or experienced abuse in the family of origin used the same form of abuse in dating relationships: "The female college student who was punched by her father is not only more likely to be abusive, but is also likely to punch her boyfriend. Her male counterpart who watched his mother throw things at her husband is not only more likely to be abusive, but is quite likely to throw things at his girlfriend" (Bernard and Bernard, 1983, p. 286).

The impact of violence between parents can be understood in more detail by examining selected individual cases. These cases convey a sense of the violent family, as viewed by children who witness episodes of physical violence and experience a generally abusive family climate.

Growing up with Spouse Abuse

Systematic, in-depth interviews and long term follow-up studies with children who have observed violence between parents are sparse. Case studies describing battered women, however, often mention children who are present in the household during battering episodes. Rouse (1986, pp. 100–101, 102) recounts two examples based on case notes from a shelter worker. These are adapted here:

> A woman, twenty-five, came in Sunday on the 5:30 A.M. bus with her three children. The two girls are three and six years old. The boy is four. Her husband has abused her since their wedding night, when he pushed her down some stairs. He has broken her collarbone, given her black eyes, and injured her back. He would not let her visit friends or go places with them. She had to be back from the store in a certain amount of time, or he would question and threaten her. He loosened the tires on her car, but her brother used the car before she did and got into an accident. They have been separated for several months, but he continues to harass her. During the last incident, he forced her to have sex with him. Two weeks ago she overdosed herself with heart medication.
>
> She has been to the shelter before. The couple started to go for

counseling, but after the second time he refused to go. He became regularly abusive, every two months or so. He would make a mess of the house and then yell at her for not keeping it clean. His family also belittles her. He degrades her. He would ask the three-year-old girl, "Should I beat your mother today or just tie her up?" He slapped one of the other children for watching cartoons, because he wanted to watch something else. He swears at his wife and says he does not care whether she comes back or not. He says he wants a divorce, but he keeps trying to get in touch with her.

The three-year-old daughter says she hates her mother and misses her father. The six-year-old is serious and aloof; at night, she cries in her sleep. The social worker involved in this case believes that the girl may have been sexually molested by the father or by a seventeen-year-old boy who was visiting the family. The four-year-old boy is angry and aggressive. He does not listen to anyone. He will walk up smiling and then just start kicking and punching anyone in his way. He screams at mealtimes, swearing and punching his mother, not eating. He will not play with the other children at the shelter. He takes toys from other children, rips the toys apart, throws them, and stomps on them. He cries when his mother is out of sight but does not cooperate with her when they are together. She tried to punish him by putting pepper in his mouth.

A woman, forty-seven, and two sons, twelve and sixteen years old, were escorted to the shelter by police at 12:30 A.M. on a Friday. The mother and the twelve-year-old were crying hard. The older boy tried to comfort his mother between telling what had happened. Her husband got angry at her when she asked him to let her drive because he was swerving all over the road. He hit her several times in the car. When they got home, he threw her around, tried to choke her, broke a table and a lamp. She fought back, striking him in the face. The sixteen-year-old hit his father and pinned him down until the police got there. The twelve-year-old hid behind a chair. The younger son was upset and scared. He said he loves his dad and wants to see him again but realizes they should move out. When not drinking, the father buys them things. Now that they have left, the boys feel maybe this time their father will change.

These two cases introduce various points of interest. First, they provide a sample of the realities of domestic violence. College personnel need to be aware of the types and severity of emotional, sexual, and physical abuse between parents, to which children may be exposed in the home. The cases also indicate how children are emotionally drawn in, even when they are not physically abused themselves (although spousal violence often spills over into a more generally dysfunctional family environment, in which children are also directly abused). The children involved display strong feelings of anger, sadness, and fear. They experience divided loyalties, helplessness, and self-blame. Identification with parents becomes conflicted. Children often feel abandoned or rejected, which contributes to an uncertain sense of self-worth. Jaffe, Wolfe, and Wilson (1990) note that children of battered women display a range of disorders, reflecting confusion, anxiety, and social isolation.

In general, such cases show that, in place of a stable, secure family environment, children may actually experience family relationships as threatening, unpredictable, and dangerous. They are learning from a highly inappropriate parental model how conflicts and stresses are handled in the family. Childhood observation of violence lays a foundation for later difficulties experienced by young adults.

As Children Grow Older

Wallerstein and Blakeslee (1989), on the basis of a ten- and fifteen-year follow-up study of divorced couples, discuss the potential damage done to children by spousal assault as they grow older. The authors note (p. 113) that "in families where children witnessed physical violence between parents, the children were not necessarily rescued by divorce." They cite the case of the Litrovskis, now divorced, and their children, including seventeen-year-old Larry:

> Larry is hostile, and ten years after the divorce, still angry. His father repeatedly beat and humiliated his mother but never hit him. He blames his mother for driving his father away; Larry's life has been worse since the divorce and he sees her as responsible. He looked up to his father and expects to "live a lot of my life just like my dad. It helps me solve my problems to drink. . . . In my relationships with girls, when I get mad I slap them, and a couple of weeks ago I hit my girlfriend on the face." His mother tells the interviewer that Larry has also threatened and attacked her: "He really hit me hard, I can't control him." Like his father, Larry belittles his mother and views her as incompetent. Larry carries these behaviors over into relationships with other women [Wallerstein and Blakeslee, 1989, pp. 114-116].

The underlying psychological process operating here appears to be identification. According to Wallerstein and Blakeslee (1989, p. 116), "by identifying with the powerful figure, the child defends him- or herself against the pain of feeling helpless." This coping mechanism can have negative consequences: "In mastering his anger and fear of a violent father, a boy can also become an oppressor" (p. 116). Long after the divorce, Larry is trapped by his childhood identification with his father, an identification reinforced by his fear of becoming like his victimized mother.

The boys in Wallerstein and Blakeslee's study who were involved in abusive relationships in late adolescence and early adulthood were all perpetrators of violence. Girls who grew up with violence between parents were sometimes perpetrators, more often victims. Wallerstein and Blakeslee describe the case of Deborah:

> Deborah was an example of a girl who seemed to be doing well until early adulthood, when she participated in a series of abusive and phys-ically violent relationships. She talked about being drawn to men with problems, finding them exciting, trying to fix these men and control them so they would not leave like her dad did. Deborah's parents fought often. She was five when her parents divorced, not long after an incident in which her father beat her mother. He never hit the children and Deborah recalls he always made the kids feel that it was her mother's fault that he hit her. Now her boyfriends are like her father. Deborah's young adult relationships appear governed by early childhood experi-ences. She realizes she is having problems with her relationships but she is not yet willing or able to change. [Wallerstein and Blakeslee, 1989, pp. 119–120].

Children's witnessing spousal violence, in a socially legitimated sexual partnership, may promote the linking of intimate relationships with vio-lence. Caring comes to mean hitting. This legacy of spousal assault will not be apparent until the child's high school and college years, when serious dating relationships typically begin. Moreover, at this age, even when stu-dents are aware at some level of recreating the type of problematic relation-ship they witnessed in childhood, they do not yet understand the dynamics involved or their own unresolved conflicts.

For perpetrators and victims alike, selective forgetting is an important defense mechanism and coping strategy. Battered women often minimize the danger to themselves of involvement in violent relationships (Rouse, 1986). Battering men are clearly characterized by denial (Gondolf, 1985); they fail to confront the seriousness of and their personal responsibility for their own domestic violence. In looking back at childhood experiences, the severity of violence witnessed may also be understated. A battering man may say, for example, that his father was a "strict disciplinarian." In fact, his father may have tied him to a chair for days, beaten him with a board, or locked him in a closet while his mother was thrown down a flight of stairs and choked to unconsciousness. Wallerstein and Blakeslee (1989) give another example of a girl, Laura, who at age fourteen dreams about a violent scene in which her father threatens her mother with a gun. She has no direct recollection of such an event, but the authors verify that when she was four she was actually present when her father threatened to kill her mother, pulled a gun, and the police came.

Counseling College Students from Violent Homes

College students carry the imprint of their family experiences. Some are still living at home with parents who have been or are still engaged in abusive behaviors; others are on their own for the first time away from home. For the most part, college students are young adults whose identities are not yet firmly established and whose competencies have yet to be proved (Roark, 1987). Nontraditional-age students are more likely to be married and may be dealing with domestic violence in their own homes. Puig (1984) notes that college adds new stresses. Those individuals who have poor relationship skills and limited social and psychological resources, and who generally deal inadequately with stress, are at higher risk of problems in college adjustment.

In counseling college students, treatment is relatively short-term, and the chief presenting complaint is not usually a family-of-origin issue. Nevertheless, the effectiveness of counseling with students from dysfunctional families could be enhanced by consideration of contributing causes, and so understanding the issues involved in domestic violence will be helpful. Jim Shadduck, a psychologist and college counselor, has provided the following three case examples:

> Mary is a twenty-three-year-old nursing student who initially requested psychotherapy for "stress." She soon revealed that she had come from a violent home and that her parents had had numerous physical fights. Mary also stated that her mother had shot her father in the shoulder during the couple's bitter custody battle for Mary and two younger siblings. Mary has been exhibiting significant anger and depression, which she relates to memories of her childhood. She also has difficulties relating to peers. Mary attended weekly sessions with a clinical psychologist for six months. She is still working on family issues, which are interfering with her academic progress.

> Fred is a twenty-seven-year-old engineering junior who requested psychotherapy to help with his marital problems. Fred has been married for nine years and has three children. He and his wife have had frequent physical conflicts for the past year, most often occurring when one or both have been drinking. On the first visit, Fred had a broken hand from hitting a wall during one of their fights, and his wife reportedly suffered a split lip and lost three front teeth when he threw a beer bottle at her. Fred and Susan both come from families with histories of alcoholism, and Fred's parents, who are now divorced, had many fights.

While Fred is concerned about his anger, drinking, and violence, he accuses Susan of provoking him. He seems alternately to be quite depressed and then to be projecting his anger and depression onto his wife. Fred and his wife went for twice weekly sessions for two months and then legally separated and were ultimately divorced.

Jane, a twenty-six-year-old sophomore political science major and her boyfriend of three years, Michael, who lives with her, received couple counseling. Jane's alcoholic father was verbally and physically abusive. He was financially supported by her mother, who accused Jane of being like her father. Jane has done well in school but remains plagued by feelings of insecurity. Jane reportedly drinks to excess several times a month and becomes abusive. Michael withholds sex when he is angry with her. Treatment focused on Jane's fears of becoming like her father and on Michael's issues of control and dependency. Jane and Michael terminated psychotherapy after four sessions, against their counselor's advice, but Jane began attending Adult Children of Alcoholics meetings.

These cases illustrate that there is no single solution for the effects of domestic violence, since the resulting feelings, attitudes, and behaviors may manifest in a variety of ways. The cases do suggest that counselors can help students confront the legacy of spouse abuse. Patterns learned in childhood can be critically examined by college students, and more positive models of interpersonal relationships can be explored. Individual counseling can provide personal insights into the psychosocial effects of growing up in a particular dysfunctional family.

Nightmares and Role Models

Psychodynamic theory and social learning theory are two perspectives drawn on in this chapter for tracing the impact of spousal abuse on children. Laura's nightmare (Wallerstein and Blakeslee, 1989) illustrates the haunting long-term psychological effect of children's witnessing violence between parents. Children are always more than passive observers. Emotionally, they are involved participants in the violent family drama, even when they are not direct targets of parental assault or battering. Children cope with such experiences in ways that may later prove to be problematic (recall the psychodynamic processes of identification and selective forgetting).

Many research studies of domestic violence support a socialization/social learning model. The family is seen as a training ground for adult relationships (Steinmetz, 1977). Use of force in response to conflicts in the family teaches that violence is an acceptable response when one is angry and frustrated or is attempting to control another person's behavior. Parents who use violence present a model of negative behavior and correspondingly fail to demonstrate positive alternatives for coping with conflict, frustration, and stress in intimate relationships (Rouse, 1984).

These two theoretical perspectives can help inform efforts to confront the legacy of spouse abuse at the college level. College personnel should be aware that spouse abuse is widespread in American society, that observation of parental violence itself victimizes children, that the long-term effects may be seen among college students, and that these effects include a variety of problematic behaviors, most notably interpersonal violence. In addition to individual counseling services, broader educational efforts are needed to address violence in relationships.

Broader Intervention Strategies

Previous writings have already provided a number of guidelines and practical suggestions for interventions with college students (for example, Puig, 1984; Bogal-Albritten and Albritten, 1985; Roscoe and Callahan, 1985; and Roark, 1987).

Awareness. Recognition of relationship violence as a serious, widespread problem is an important first step. Bogal-Albritten and Albritten (1985) obtained completed questionnaires from 345 housing directors and 228 counseling directors, as well as from 510 students, and found that few institutions responding to the survey cited specific policies for dealing with courtship violence. Roscoe and Callahan (1985) listed the need for greater awareness of this problem as one of the most urgent implications of their findings on courtship violence among adolescents.

Campus Surveys. Evidence of abusive family backgrounds and subsequent relationship violence among students at one's own college can be gathered through a campus survey. Among college students, an estimated 20 percent of premarital dating includes incidents of violent behavior (Makepeace, 1981). The most common and frequent modes of interpersonal violence among students are likely to be hitting, slapping, punching, shoving, and pushing, but numerous cases of even the less frequent and more severe types of violence are bound to occur in a large student body. Documentation of local occurrences and of the negative effects of intimate violence among students verifies the need for services and helps to motivate program planning.

Campuswide Education. Targets of educational efforts should include various administrators, residence hall staff, counselors, health services staff, campus police, faculty, and students. Information should be made available on how to identify an abusive relationship, why violence occurs, why partners stay in abusive relationships, who may be an abuser, who is being abused, and so on. Workshops, guest lectures, posters, brochures, featured campus speakers, and campus newspaper articles are techniques for communicating this information. After initial development of resources, publicity campaigns should be undertaken periodically, to remind the college community of the problem and highlight available resources.

Support Systems. Services suggested include links with a shelter for battered women, rape assistance programs, and any other existing community resources. A readily identified, accessible support system for students who live on and off campus is important, incorporating individual counseling services, peer-support groups, and appropriate referrals. Roark (1987) recommends development of coordinated services through a college or university committee representing all sectors of the campus—administrators, faculty, and students, as well as staff. This procedure allows various perspectives to be shared and promotes a broad-based collective commitment to program implementation.

Skill Building. A component on domestic violence can be added to existing skill-building programs. Workshop leaders can address causes, change attitudes, and help develop coping mechanisms in workshops on leadership; assertiveness; self-esteem; values clarification; sexual decision making; self-defense; anger management; conflict resolution; stress management; alcohol education; rape prevention; human relations; relationship enhancement; social-skills training; and so on. A variety of source materials are available for adoption or modification. For example, Puig (1984) describes a ninety-minute didactic seminar and audiovisual presentation conducted by two leaders—a counseling center psychologist, and a campus law enforcement officer. A brief questionnaire is used to make participants aware of the incidence of and myths about partner abuse, with time allotted for questions and comments. A film about battered women is shown and discussed. At the end, there is a review of resources available to students, including campus police and counseling services.

Conclusion

Wider acknowledgment of relationship violence is a crucial component of effective college interventions. Eliminating ignorance about domestic violence means no longer viewing abusive actions between partners as a private issue and lifting the silence that gives implicit consent (Puig, 1984). Roark (1987), too, notes that one of the factors contributing to violence among college students is society's seeming legitimation of intimate violence insofar as such actions are condoned, excused, or ignored. Roscoe and Callahan (1985) emphasize the need for all college personnel to communicate an unambiguous message that violence is a pervasive but undesirable and unnecessary aspect of interpersonal relationships.

Campus police and residence hall staff are the persons most likely to be responding directly to incidents of sexual and physical assault. Most college personnel will not witness acts of violence in relationships, but they will see the consequences when a student's learning environment (which extends beyond the classroom) is disrupted and his or her personal development is undermined. Observers may not connect these negative effects with family and dating violence. Students themselves may not see a connection or may be reluctant to raise the issue. If, however, questions about family and dating violence are routinely asked, students are given "permission to talk about violence and see the problem as a legitimate one" (Jaffe, Wolfe, and Wilson, 1990, p. 101).

College counselors play an important role in treating individual students for harm already done by childhood exposure to family violence. Habits of denial or other ineffective coping strategies can be challenged, a nonabusive relationship can be modeled, and skills can be taught, to allow more constructive responses to conflict and stress. The potential negative impact, not widely understood, of simply witnessing violence between parents can be validated for students. When treatment is effective, students are able to see how family violence has influenced them and can modify their own behavior patterns, so that the cycle of intergenerational transmission can be broken.

In addition to providing and making referrals for individual treatment, college personnel are concerned with prevention—inhibiting further violence and victimization. Advocacy for preventive interventions is an area in which college personnel can provide leadership. Fortunately, according to Roark (1987, p. 370) prevention of campus violence "depends not so much on discovering unique new approaches as commitment to already known approaches. . . . The mechanisms necessary to counteract violence are already generally available." College students' development is already an accepted goal, and it can be recognized as specifically including the creation of mature adults who do not accept violence as appropriate behavior. New cases can be prevented "by addressing causes and changing actions, attitudes and values relating to the conditions that foster violence" (Roark, 1987, p. 368).

To summarize, college students from dysfunctional families in which they witnessed spouse abuse were affected by violence in the family, even when they were not direct victims of assault. The long-term effects are seen among college students in their own abusive relationships, personal turmoil, and problems with college adjustment. The psychodynamic and social learning theories, among others, help to explain the psychological trauma, skills deficiencies, and interpersonal problems created by observation of violence between parents. College personnel have opportunities to undo the negative legacy of spouse abuse by means of a wide range of intervention strategies, including individual counseling and broader educational efforts.

References

Bernard, M. L., and Bernard, T. L. "Violent Intimacy: The Family as a Model for Love Relationships." *Family Relations*, 1983, 32, 283–286.

Bogal-Albritten, R. B., and Albritten, W. L. "The Hidden Victims: Courtship Violence Among College Students." *Journal of College Student Personnel*, 1985, *26*, 201-204.

Flynn, J. "Recent Findings Related to Wife Abuse." *Social Casework*, 1977, *58* (1), 13-20.

Gondolf, E. W. *Men Who Batter.* Holmes Beach, Fla.: Learning Publications, 1985.

Hotaling, G. T., Finkelhor, D., Kirkpatrick, J. T., and Straus, M. (eds.). *Family Abuse and Its Consequences.* Newbury Park, Calif.: Sage, 1988.

Jaffe, P. G., Wolfe, D. E., and Wilson, S. K. *Children of Battered Women.* Newbury Park, Calif.: Sage, 1990.

Makepeace, J. M. "Courtship Violence Among College Students." *Family Relations*, 1981, *30*, 97-102.

O'Brien, J. E. "Violence in Divorce Prone Families." *Journal of Marriage and the Family*, 1971, *33* (4), 692-697.

Puig, A. "Predomestic Strife: A Growing College Counseling Concern." *Journal of College Student Personnel*, 1984, *25*, 268-269.

Roark, M. L. "Preventing Violence on College Campuses." *Journal of Counseling and Development*, 1987, *65*, 367-371.

Roscoe, B., and Callahan, J. E. "Adolescents' Self-Report of Violence in Families and Dating Relationships." *Adolescence*, 1985, *20* (79), 545-553.

Rouse, L. P. "Models, Self-Esteem and Locus of Control as Factors Contributing to Spouse Abuse." *Victimology*, 1984, *9* (1), 130-141.

Rouse, L. P. *You Are Not Alone: A Guide for Battered Women.* Holmes Beach, Fla.: Learning Publications, 1986.

Rouse, L. P., Breen, R., and Howell, M. "Abuse in Intimate Relationships: A Comparison of Married and Dating College Students." *Journal of Interpersonal Violence*, 1988, *3* (4), 414-429.

Steinmetz, S. K. "The Use of Force for Resolving Family Conflict: The Training Ground for Abuse." *Family Co-ordinator*, 1977, *26*, 19-26.

Steinmetz, S. K., and Straus, M. A. "The Family as a Cradle of Violence." *Society*, 1973, *10*, 50-56.

Straus, M. A. "Measuring Intrafamily Conflict and Violence: The Conflict Tactics Scales." *Journal of Marriage and the Family*, 1979, *41*, 75-88.

Wallerstein, J. S., and Blakeslee, S. *Second Chances: Men, Women, and Children a Decade After Divorce.* New York: Ticknor & Fields, 1989.

Linda P. Rouse is associate professor of sociology in the Department of Sociology, Anthropology and Social Work at the University of Texas, Arlington.

This chapter describes the dynamics of childhood sexual abuse,
identifies the prevalence of college-student sexual abuse survivors,
and addresses the major issues of child sexual abuse as they
relate to college students.

College-Student Survivors of Incest and Other Child Sexual Abuse

Robert I. Witchel

Since the late 1970s, incest and other forms of child sexual abuse have been a focus of attention for professionals concerned about the well-being of children. Changing laws, significant attention from the media, the creation of sexual abuse prevention programs, and the development of treatment and support services have contributed to the explosion of disclosures from children and adults (including college students) about memories of childhood sexual abuse. Child sexual abuse often remains secret and can disrupt personal development and trigger a lifetime of suffering. All aspects of life can be affected because sexual abuse not only is sexually intrusive but can also make an emotional, physical, and spiritual impact on the child.

This chapter provides an overview of childhood sexual abuse and identifies the prevalence of survivors among college students. The major issues faced by survivors on campus are addressed and illustrated by case examples. A review of the results of a survey of college students explores the impact of childhood sexual abuse on students' current life functioning. The chapter concludes with recommendations to college campuses for developing more effective responses.

Child Sexual Abuse: An Overview

National statistics have indicated that 100,000 to 500,000 children are sexually abused each year. Prevalence rates for child sexual abuse derived from various North American studies have ranged from 6 percent to 62 percent for females and from 3 percent to 31 percent for males (Peters, Wyatt, and Finkelhor, 1986). Studies of prevalence rates among college

NEW DIRECTIONS FOR STUDENT SERVICES, no. 54, Summer 1991 © Jossey-Bass Inc., Publishers

students date back to Landis (1956), who in a survey of 1,800 college students found 30 percent of males and 35 percent of females reporting an abuse experience. More recent surveys demonstrate prevalence rates among college students to be consistent with rates among noncollege populations (Finkelhor, 1979; Sedney and Brooks, 1984; Fromuth, 1986). Bass and Davis (1988, p. 20) state, "One out of three girls, and one out of seven boys, are sexually abused by the time they reach the age of eighteen."

Definitions. Child sexual abuse is a sexual act imposed on a child or adolescent by force or manipulation, where there is an imbalance in age, size, power, or knowledge. The abuser is often a family member (immediate or extended) or an acquaintance. Incest, from a legal and mental health perspective, pertains to sexual activity between a child and a parent or other family member—for example, an uncle, a grandparent, or a sibling. Blume, however, offers a new definition of incest as "the imposition of sexually inappropriate acts, or acts with sexual overtones, by—or any use of a minor child to meet the sexual or sexual/emotional needs of—one or more persons who derive authority through an ongoing emotional bonding with that child" (Blume, 1990, p. 4). This definition extends the concept of the "family sexual abuse" experience to anyone the child relies or depends on such as a teacher, a clergyman, a neighbor, a coach, or a family friend.

Types. Sexual abuse includes a wide range of behaviors, from fondling and exhibition to sexual intercourse and sexual exploitation (using children for prostitution or pornography). Sgroi (1982) offers a progression of abusive behaviors, which further describes the types of sexual abuse. Bass and Davis (1988) ask readers a number of questions about their experiences as children, to determine whether they were victims of sexual abuse.

Effects. The effects of sexual abuse include but are not limited to depression, self-destructive behavior, anxiety, feelings of isolation, low self-esteem, substance abuse, and vulnerability toward revictimization. Referring to abused boys, Hunter (1990 p. 45) writes, "Naturally, each person is unique and will react in his own way, based on the personality and personal resources he had prior to the onset of the abuse." Additional factors, unrelated to personality, have been identified as determinants of the impact of abuse. These include the child's age when the abuse began, the length and frequency of the abuse, the severity of the sexual acts, the level of threat and violence, the child's relationship to the perpetrator, the number of perpetrators, and the manner in which other adults in the child's life responded to the child, even if they were unaware of the abuse (Blume, 1990; Russell, 1986; Sgroi, 1988).

College-Student Survivors of Sexual Abuse: Prevalence

Twenty-five years ago, through a survey of 1,200 college females, Gagnon (1965) found that 28 percent reported sexual experience with an adult before age thirteen. Only 6 percent of the students reporting sexual abuse recalled the event being reported to the police, and for 21 percent the report to the interviewer was the student's first time telling anyone of the abuse. Gagnon's study supports the belief that incest and other forms of child sexual abuse are not a recent phenomenon but have historically affected college students. The study also illustrates that child sexual abuse often remains secret, causing internal distress for college-student survivors.

More recent studies continue to support the high prevalence of incest/sexual abuse survivors within the college population (Finkelhor, 1979; Fromuth, 1986; Sedney and Brooks, 1984; Seidner, and Calhoun, 1984; Witchel, 1989). Finkelhor's (1979) sample was drawn from six New England colleges and showed a 19.2 percent prevalence rate of child sexual abuse among women and 8.6 percent among men. Fromuth (1986) found that 22 percent of 482 college women, a rate comparable to Finklehor's, reported at least one sexually abusive relationship during childhood. Witchel (1989) received questionnaires from 1,577 college students and found that 530 (34 percent) students recalled an experience of sexual abuse before age sixteen with someone at least five years older (results from this study are reported later in this chapter).

Lack of Family Support

As indicated in Chapter One, the family support system has been identified as a critical ingredient of the student's positive transition to college. According to Utain and Oliver (1989, p. 207), "Like all dysfunctional families, the incest family suffers from poor communications within the family, poor links to the external environment, rigid rules and low self-esteem of family members." College-student incest survivors have been influenced by this unhealthy life-style and often perceive the family not as a stable, reliable source of comfort but as a source of pain and confusion. Survivors who were never able to disclose the abuse to their families, or who did not receive the needed support when they did disclose, probably came from more dysfunctional families. Sexual abuse survivors growing up in dysfunctional families are likely to lack the support and nurturance identified as critical to college adjustment.

Impacts on Students' Development

A history of sexual abuse can block students as they confront the developmental challenges of the college years. A survivor's attempts to develop positive feelings about self, productive relationships with others, and healthy life skills are often hindered by unresolved memories of sexual abuse.

Identity. Chickering (1969) believes that establishing identity is dependent on the preceding vectors of achieving competence, managing emotions, and becoming autonomous. This serves as a springboard for the subsequent vectors of freeing interpersonal relationships, clarifying purposes, and developing integrity. Childhood sexual abuse survivors may have significant difficulties in completing early vectors. This causes challenges to identity development and can result in problems with developing interpersonal relationships, purpose, and integrity. The focus on early sexuality tends to interfere with the accomplishment of the developmental tasks of childhood and adolescence, thus creating obstacles to a student's ability to achieve the developmental tasks of young adulthood. Chickering identifies conceptions concerning body and appearance as an important part of identity development. Sexual abuse survivors often have a self-perception of being "damaged goods," resulting from actual physical injury, pain during sexual abuse, and/or reactions from others about the abuse (Sgroi, 1982). Survivors are often concerned about physical impairment, referring to themselves in derogatory terms and finding themselves unappealing. According to Sgroi (1982, p. 125), "The bottom line is that child sexual abuse involves a violation of the victim's body, privacy, and rights of self-mastery and control." As a result of a negative physical self-concept and concerns over sexual identity, the important aspects of identity, as identified by Chickering (1969), can suffer impairment.

Needs. The impact of sexual abuse on personality development can be examined with the hierarchical model of motivation proposed by Maslow (1970). The lower-level needs in the human hierarchy are the satisfaction of bodily and safety needs and the sense of belonging. These needs must be satisfied before the higher-order needs, such as esteem, can be focused on by the person. The act of sexual abuse often controls the child, thus creating frustration in his or her attempts to fulfill physiological needs, such as bodily integrity, and safety needs, including security, stability, and protection. The sexually abusive relationship would be likely to frustrate the child in the pursuit of healthy love and a sense of belonging. Lack of fulfillment of the lower-level needs creates significant challenges to the person faced with satisfying esteem needs—for example, independence, desire for competence and achievement, self-confidence, and mastery of oneself and one's environment. Young adults are involved in a process of developing autonomy, seeking mature interpersonal relationships, and creating purpose—tasks that appear related to Maslow's higher-order needs. Survivors of child sexual abuse may need to attend to lower-level needs by repairing the damage caused by the abuse before attempting to satisfy higher-order needs.

Sexuality. Maltz and Holman (1987, p. 4) believe that "a person's sexuality is significantly affected by the experience of childhood sexual abuse." Early sexual experiences strongly influence sexual attitudes and behaviors and foster inaccurate beliefs about sexuality. Survivors were not allowed to make their own choices about sexuality and often confuse sexual abuse with sexuality.

The addition of a history of sexual abuse creates a more complex situation for college students as they face struggles and pressures related to decisions about sexual and intimate behavior. Finkelhor (1979) found that college-student sexual abuse survivors had significantly lower levels of sexual self-esteem than their nonabused classmates did. In a campus environment where sexual intimacy is often an expectation on the first date, survivors of sexual abuse experience a variety of difficulties. The effects of sexual abuse on students' sexual choices can include an overactive or self-destructive sexual life-style, sexual withdrawal due to fear and lack of trust, an inability to say no and set limits, submitting to any initiation of sex, an inability to enjoy intimate contact, and an aversion to certain sexual experiences that evoke memories of the abuse.

Sexual abuse survivors may also question their sexual identity. Female incest survivors may experience difficulties in heterosexual relationships and choose female partners (Maltz and Holman, 1987). A young male survivor abused by an older male may question his sexual orientation, interpreting the abuse incidents as evidence of a sexual preference for males (Finkelhor, 1984). Survivors may become fearful, angry, and untrusting of others who are the same sex as the perpetrator, and these emotions may affect choices about sexual preference. A clearer understanding of the relationship between child sexual abuse and sexual preference requires further research.

In summary, the impact of sexual abuse on a student's early development creates frustrations as the student confronts the developmental challenges of the college years. A survivor can be hampered by a poorly developed identity, feelings of insecurity, social isolation, and lack of trust in others.

Effects on College Students

Browne and Finkelhor (1986, p. 162), in a review of research on the long-term effects of sexual abuse, say that "adult women victimized as children are more likely [than women not victimized as children] to manifest depression, self-destructive behavior, anxiety, feelings of isolation and stigma, poor self-esteem, a tendency toward revictimization, and substance abuse." Similar effects are described by Lew (1988) for male victims of sexual abuse. This section explores the relationship between a history of childhood sexual abuse and such critical concerns as vulnerability to coercive sex, alcohol and other drug use, and suicide attempts. Case examples are used to illustrate the dynamics of sexual abuse and its impact on college students. These cases represent real students, whose names and identifying data have been changed to maintain their privacy. Results from the author's recent study are also reported.

Vulnerability. Many survivors experience a sense of powerlessness about sexuality, resulting in a learned vulnerability in relationships that allows for susceptibility to further abusive experiences, such as date rape, sexual harassment, and abusive or battering relationships. Survivors who experience forced sexual interaction will often have flashbacks to the childhood sexual abuse, displaying such responses as fear, panic, rage, automatic submission, and/or dissociation from the present experience.

An example of learned vulnerability is coercive sex, including date rape and sexual harassment, which is an increasingly serious problem on college and university campuses. Studies of community women (Russell, 1986) and college women (Fromuth, 1986) offer evidence that childhood sexual abuse is related to later being a victim of coercive sex. In a study conducted by Witchel (1989), comparing sexually abused and nonabused college students, subjects were asked to indicate the number of times in the past twelve months that they had been coerced into performing sexual acts. Thirty-five percent of abused students and 15 percent of nonabused students reported being sexually coerced on one or more occasions. These results indicate that sexual abuse survivors are more vulnerable to being coerced into unwanted sexual activities.

> Sally was sexually assaulted by three teenaged boys in her neighborhood, beginning at the age of nine. During the first incident, Sally was forced to engage in oral sex with the three boys. Subsequent incidents involved one or more of the boys and, although Sally never told anyone about the abuse, she put a stop to it when she turned twelve. During Sally's freshman year of college, she developed a friendship with a man who lived in her residence hall. While talking one evening, this man began to make sexual advances toward Sally. She panicked because the incident triggered many old feelings and fears related to the prior abuse. Sally was unable to stop him and she again was forced to engage in oral sex. This assault set off a chain of events for Sally, which included her temporarily dropping out of school. Sally entered counseling and was able to identify issues related to the recent incident, as well as the abuse experienced as a child. Sally's history of abuse, and the fact that she never discussed the childhood incidents with anyone, contributed to her vulnerability to coercive sex.

Alcohol and Other Drug Use. Substances can play a role in the life of the sexual abuse survivor in a number of ways. The abuser and other family members may have had problems with alcohol or other drugs. Alcohol may have been used as a disinhibitor, allowing the abuser to disregard taboos against sexual involvement with children. The survivor, too, may have used alcohol or other drugs as a means of coping with the pain and other effects associated with the abuse. College-student survivors may use alcohol and other drugs as a form of self-medication to deal with unpleasant feelings and memories. The increased availability of substances on college campuses creates risks for the sexual abuse survivor, especially the student who has developed a pattern of overuse. Hussey and Singer (1989, pp. 53–54) summarize information from adolescents admitted to an inpatient psychiatric unit: "The data show that, in our population, adolescents who have been sexually abused had more harmful substance use patterns, had more frequently sought professional help for drinking, had a greater incidence of blackouts, and perceived getting more benefits from taking drugs than adolescents not known to suffer from such abuse." Briere (1984) found that 27 percent of childhood sexual abuse victims had a history of alcoholism (compared with 11 percent of nonvictims), and 21 percent had a history of drug addiction (compared to 2 percent of the nonvictims).

In the present author's study, students were asked to indicate how often during the past twelve months they had used drugs (marijuana, cocaine, crack, LSD). Even though the size of the abused sample was less than half the number of nonabused students, the sexually abused students represented more than 50 percent of students indicating that they used drugs often or very often. Results indicate that a frequent pattern of drug use may reflect a history of sexual abuse. In regard to alcohol use, no differences were found between the two groups, a result similar to that reported by Sedney and Brooks (1984).

Ron was sexually abused by two uncles on an ongoing basis, beginning at age four and continuing through age sixteen, when he aggressively resisted. The abuse involved fondling, mutual masturbation, oral sex, and anal penetration. Ron described entering college as "the first time in my life I was free from it, and I knew I couldn't be touched in that way." During his freshman year, Ron became a "full-fledged alcohol abuser" and admitted this was his means of "drowning out" painful memories of the abuse. Ron's alcohol use declined during his sophomore year, his grades improved, and he worked at two part-time jobs.

Ron's dad was an alcoholic, and his parents were divorced after years of violence; emotional and financial support from home was minimal. Ron described a need to be "restrained and guarded" around people, not revealing too much. His anger for other males (or repressed anger toward his uncles) was bubbling below the surface, and he reported angry outbursts. The abuse resulted in confusing messages about love and trust, creating problems for Ron in his relationships with women. Ron usually ended relationships to avoid getting hurt; his alcohol use increased at these times. He shared this self-appraisal: "When I am with someone who gives and can receive, there is no problem, but when the other person is only into receiving, it's a real problem." He believes this stemmed from being manipulated into "giving" to his uncles.

Ron experienced much confusion about his sexual orientation and was concerned about becoming an abuser himself, but he did not fully acknowledge these issues until he entered therapy, three years after graduation. After eighteen months of therapy, Ron described himself as "satisfied with resolving my abuse. I can't change any of it; I can live with it, accept it, and perhaps make something good out of it." Ron, now twenty-seven, is a journalist, married, and a father.

Ron faced the usual challenges of college, with the added struggles often faced by sexual abuse victims from alcoholic families. He used alcohol during high school, and in his freshman year of college it offered temporary relief from pain and confusion. He dealt privately with his inner turmoil about the abuse because he had faithfully maintained the secret. Ron struggled with confusion about his sexual orientation, fears of becoming an abuser himself, and failures in relationships. Ron's alcohol-related behavior sent signals to members of the university community that he was in trouble, but his own repression of memories of abuse, coupled with the lack of effective interventions on the part of others, allowed him to continue to suffer in silence.

Suicide Attempts. The present author's study asked students to indicate the number of times they had attempted suicide during the past twelve months. Three percent of the nonabused students and 7 percent of the abused students reported making one or more suicide attempts. Even though the size of the abused population was less than half the number of nonabused students, the sexually abused students were responsible for 64 percent of reported suicide attempts. Therefore, sexually abused students reported more suicide attempts than their nonabused peers did.

Sue was a victim of incest by her stepfather, who began to fondle her when she was eight years old. By age eleven, the abuse included oral sex and vaginal penetration and occurred up to five times per week. The abuse continued until Sue left for college, although it was less frequent during her senior year because she often made attempts to be out of the house. Sue had not told anyone about the abuse before entering college, since her stepfather had threatened to kill her and her mother if she did.

Sue had buried herself in her schoolwork throughout high school, never dated, had few close friends, and generally felt depressed and defeated. She had made numerous attempts at suicide during high school, but only one friend knew about them. Sue thought college was her one chance to escape, and she chose a campus about one hour from her home. Sue lived alone in an off-campus residence. One late evening, her stepfather came to visit. He had been drinking as was often the case. He pressured Sue into having sex with him, leaving her devastated because she had felt that she was finally safe from him. After he left, she felt angry, depressed, and fearful that the abuse was beginning all over again.

Sue's stepfather continued to visit her about once a month, and the pattern of abuse continued. His threats kept her from disclosing the abuse, but finally, out of desperation, she told a faculty member about it. Sue made another suicide attempt, which resulted in an overnight hospital stay. A social worker spoke with her, and she agreed to meet with a counseling center psychologist who specialized in treatment of sexual abuse. Exposing the history of the abuse was painful but brought relief. The most important but most difficult step was meeting with the police and pressing charges against her stepfather. Another important step was revealing the long-term abuse to her mother and her family and managing the aftermath that often comes with such disclosure. As Sue began treatment, stopping her stepfather's behavior was a critical first step in her recovery.

Sue experienced a full range of problems as a result of the abuse. Burying herself in her schoolwork, reducing her time at home during her senior year, and leaving home to attend college served as partial escapes from the abuse. Her stepfather, however, whose behavior was still protected by secrecy, risked continuing to abuse Sue while she was at college. With support from a university staff member, she was able to find the resources to stop the abuse and begin a recovery process.

Eating Difficulties. Bass and Davis (1988, p. 50) state, "Eating difficulties often result from abuse. Young girls who were sexually abused sometimes develop anorexia and bulimia." When sexual abuse is ongoing and hidden, the anorexia or bulimia may be a cry for help. These eating patterns may also represent a way of saying no, and they may be the only choice the adolescent believes she has to exert control over her life (Bass and Davis, 1988). In the present author's study, students were asked to indicate how often in the past twelve months they had experienced symptoms related to anorexia, bulimia, or excessive overeating. Thirty-one percent of sexually abused students and 21 percent of nonabused students reported having had these symptoms. Even though the size of the abused population was less than half the number of nonabused students, the sexually abused students represented 54 percent of those students who indicated experiencing symptoms very often.

Jan was sexually abused at age five by her older brother, who was thirteen. The sexual incidents began with fondling and progressed to oral sex and intercourse. The incidents occurred on a regular basis for five years, until her brother left for college. When he returned for holidays and summer vacations, further incidents took place. As Jan turned twelve, she began to experience symptoms of bulimia. During her teenage years her symptoms grew worse and were noticed by her parents. A physician's examination resulted in referral to an eating disorders treatment program. At times Jan's symptoms would diminish, but when she experienced stress they would increase. By the time Jan entered college, she had experienced numerous hospitalizations and long-term psychotherapy related to her bulimia; however, she had never disclosed, nor had she been asked about, sexual abuse. During her first year in college, she experienced the usual stresses of the freshman year, and this resulted in another increase in symptoms. Her resident assistant became concerned and referred her to the counseling center. Toward the end of her initial interview, the counselor asked, "Who sexually abused you?" Jan's response was "Let me tell you about the story of my life," and she began the painful but relieving process of disclosing the abuse. For the first time, Jan began to confront the real issues underlying her bulimia. Another important issue was the fact that Jan's brother, during college vacations, continued to molest Jan. (Gathering further information about Jan's brother would raise issues about an incest offender's adjustment to college.)

In summary, recognizing a relationship between a history of childhood sexual abuse and such concerns as coercive sex, suicide attempts, eating disorders, and drug use is critical for student affairs professionals, faculty, and administrators. One common thread in these case examples is the inability of the family to offer the necessary qualities (trust, openness, support) to intervene in the silent struggle experienced by the child or adolescent victim. College professionals are often in a position to make a more healthy intervention. The next section describes a campuswide plan.

A Challenge for College Campuses

Responding effectively to the needs and challenges of childhood sexual abuse survivors requires a comprehensive plan, including staff training, education programs, intervention strategies, and counseling and support services. Administrators, student affairs professionals, and faculty need expertise in the issues of sexual abuse in order to provide the leadership to develop and implement a campuswide program. Staff working in residence halls, counseling centers, health services, judicial systems, alcohol and drug programs, and learning centers are in strategic positions to respond to survivors of sexual abuse. Current programs and services, designed to address needs related to alcohol and other drug use, suicide prevention, sexual harassment, courtship violence, eating disorders, rape prevention, and human sexuality, need to include an exploration of childhood sexual abuse issues.

Training. Childhood sexual abuse survivors' needs require special skills and sensitivities from student affairs professionals, faculty, administrators, and student paraprofessionals throughout the campus. A significant step is to design and offer awareness workshops to professional staff, faculty, and student paraprofessionals (such as resident assistants and peer counselors). These workshops may trigger emotional reactions in participants, especially those who are themselves survivors of sexual abuse. Facilitators need to be available to offer support and referrals to other resources. The following objectives for training are suggested:

To increase awareness of the prevalence of childhood sexual abuse survivors on campus

To develop an awareness of the symptoms of sexual abuse often exhibited by college students

To recognize the relationship between a history of childhood sexual abuse and suicide attempts, depression, drug use, date rape, and other relationship violence

To develop intervention skills and learn how and when to ask, "Were you ever sexually abused as a child?"

To develop an awareness of existing sexual abuse counseling and support services and referral procedures.

Educational Programs. It is important to provide sexual abuse awareness programs in a variety of campus settings and to various student groups, such as freshmen, fraternity and sorority members, student government representatives, and peer counselors. Most campuses provide educational programs focusing on rape prevention, eating disorders, drug abuse, sexuality, and a wide range of personal growth issues. Information about sexual abuse can be integrated into many of these existing programs, as well as into specific educational programs on childhood sexual abuse. Providing sex education and awareness programs designed to foster more responsible sexual decision-making behavior can be valuable for all students, but especially for sexual abuse survivors. Programs of this type often attract survivors, many of whom have not previously disclosed the abuse. These student survivors may experience a variety of emotional reactions to a presentation, requiring sensitive presenters who can offer additional support and resources. Survivors frequently remain after the program and attempt to have some personal contact with the presenter. This is an excellent opportunity to establish some trust and offer support.

Intervention. As students present concerns about depression, suicide, drug use, date rape, eating disorders, and other issues described in this chapter, it is important to explore what role, if any, childhood sexual abuse may have played. These crisis points, as illustrated in some of the case examples, often provide an opportunity to ask students about memories of sexual abuse. In situations related to coercive sex or courtship violence, a student can be asked, "Did something like this ever happen to you before?" In situations related to depression or attempted suicide, the student can be asked, "Were there other times in your life when you felt like this?" A referral to sexual abuse counseling professionals is an important step in the intervention process.

Counseling. Counseling centers provide services to students presenting many of the concerns identified throughout this chapter. A substantial percentage of these students are likely to be survivors of sexual abuse. The student may not have shared the abuse during counseling, however, or the counselor may not have explored the possibility of sexual abuse. A student's progress in counseling is likely to be limited if memories of sexual abuse are repressed or ignored by the counselor.

Campus counseling agencies need to assess whether they can offer sexual abuse treatment services. Therapy for survivors can often be a long-term process and, because many counseling centers limit the number of counseling sessions, referral to off-campus sexual abuse treatment specialists may be more practical and ethical. Moreover, since sexual abuse treatment has quickly become a specialty area, student survivors can have access to professionals, either on or off campus, who will assess and focus on their specific treatment needs. If a campus decides to offer services, professional staff providing such services need to explore their own attitudes and feelings about child sexual abuse and obtain specific sexual abuse treatment skills. A number of recently developed resources (Bass and Davis, 1988; Blume, 1990; Courtois, 1988; Poston and Lison, 1989; Utain and Oliver, 1989) provide useful healing strategies to counselors and survivors. In general, these resources identify the following recovery goals:

1. To express feelings about the sexual abuse and the abuser
2. To understand the sexual abuse in ways that are not destructive to the self-image
3. To reduce the sense of responsibility and guilt for the abuse
4. To recognize the negative impact that the sexual abuse has had on feelings about the self and on relationships with others
5. To learn more assertive behaviors and communication skills in sexual and nonsexual situations
6. To develop more appropriate ways of expressing and meeting needs
7. To learn more healthy life skills, such as decision making and limit setting.

Summary

College and university staff, faculty, and student affairs professionals need to recognize the prevalence of childhood sexual abuse survivors on campus and the impact made by the abuse. As students present concerns about suicide and depression, drug use, coercive sex, eating disorders, and other crises, an exploration of the role that childhood sexual abuse may have played is important. Responding effectively to the needs and challenges of childhood sexual abuse survivors requires college professionals to develop a comprehensive plan that includes staff training, educational programs, intervention strategies, and counseling services.

References

Bass, E., and Davis, L. *The Courage to Heal: A Guide for Women Survivors of Child Sexual Abuse.* New York: Harper & Row, 1988.

Blume, E. S. *Secret Survivors: Uncovering Incest and Its Aftereffects in Women.* New York: Wiley, 1990.

Briere, J. "The Long-Term Effects of Childhood Sexual Abuse: Defining a Post-Sexual-Abuse Syndrome." Paper presented at the Third National Conference on Sexual Victimization of Children, Washington, D.C., Apr. 1984.

Browne, A., and Finkelhor, D. "Initial and Long-Term Effects: A Review of the Research. " In D. Finkelhor (ed.), *A Sourcebook of Child Sexual Abuse.* Newbury Park, Calif.: Sage, 1986.

Chickering, A. W. *Education and Identity.* San Francisco: Jossey-Bass, 1969.

Courtois, C. *Healing the Incest Wound: Adult Survivors in Therapy.* New York: Norton, 1988.

Finkelhor, D. *Sexually Victimized Children.* New York: Free Press, 1979.

Finkelhor, D. *Child Sexual Abuse: New Theory and Research.* New York: Free Press, 1984.

Fromuth, M. E. "The Relationship of Childhood Sexual Abuse with Later Psychological and Sexual Adjustment in a Sample of College Women." *Child Abuse and Neglect,* 1986, *10,* 5-15.

Gagnon, J. "Female Child Victims of Sexual Offense." *Social Problems,* 1965, *13,* 176-192.

Hunter, M. *Abused Boys: The Neglected Victims of Sexual Abuse.* Lexington, Mass.: Heath, 1990.

Hussey, D., and Singer, M. "Innovations in the Assessment and Treatment of Sexually Abused Adolescents: An Inpatient Model." In S. M. Sgroi (ed.), *Vulnerable Populations.* Vol. 2. Lexington, Mass.: Heath, 1989.

Landis, J. "Experiences of 500 Children with Adult Sexual Deviants." *Psychiatric Quarterly Supplement,* 1956, *30,* 91-109.

Lew, M. *Victims No Longer: Men Recovering from Incest and Other Sexual Child Abuse.* New York: Nevraumont, 1988.

Maltz, W., and Holman, B. *Incest and Sexuality: A Guide to Understanding and Healing.* Lexington, Mass.: Heath, 1987.

Maslow, A. H. *Motivation and Personality.* (2nd ed.) New York: Harper & Row, 1970.

Miller, B., and Marshall, J. "Coercive Sex on the University Campus." *Journal of College Student Personnel,* 1987, *28* (1), 38-47.

Peters, S. D., Wyatt, G. E., and Finkelhor, D. "Prevalence." In D. Finkelhor (ed.), *A Sourcebook of Child Sexual Abuse.* Newbury Park, Calif.: Sage, 1986.

Poston, C., and Lison, K. *Reclaiming Our Lives: Hope for Adult Survivors of Incest.* Boston: Little, Brown, 1989.

Russell, D. *The Secret Trauma: Incest in the Lives of Girls and Women.* New York: Basic Books, 1986.

Sedney, M. A., and Brooks, B. "Factors Associated with a History of Childhood Sexual Experience in a Nonclinical Female Population." *Journal of the American Academy of Child Psychiatry,* 1984, *23,* 215-218.

Seidner, A. L., and Calhoun, K. S. "Childhood Sexual Abuse: Factors Related to Differential Adult Adjustment." Paper presented at the Second National Conference for Family Violence Researchers, Durham, N.H., Aug. 1984.

Sgroi, S. M. (ed.). *Handbook of Clinical Intervention in Child Sexual Abuse.* Lexington, Mass.: Lexington Books, 1982.

Sgroi, S. M. (ed.). *Vulnerable Populations.* Vol. 1. Lexington, Mass.: Heath, 1988.

Utain, M., and Oliver, B. *Scream Louder: Through Hell and Healing with an Incest Survivor and Her Therapist.* Deerfield Beach, Fla.: Health Communications, 1989.

Witchel, R. I. "Child Sexual Abuse and College Students' Life Functioning: Focusing Our Vision." Paper presented at the annual conference of the American College Personnel Association, Washington, D.C., Mar. 1989.

Robert I. Witchel is chair of the Department of Counselor Education at Indiana University of Pennsylvania. As a former counseling center director on two campuses, Dr. Witchel has worked extensively with high-risk college students from dysfunctional families. As a licensed psychologist, he has provided therapy to families experiencing difficulties with divorce and child custody, child abuse, alcohol abuse, and other forms of family dysfunction.

Some students have dedicated their entire lives to denying, to themselves and to the world, that they were neglected. Through all their accomplishments they have been seen but never heard.

College Students from Emotionally Neglectful Homes

Donelda A. Cook

Experts estimate that from 80 to 85 percent of people have experienced some form of neglect during their childhood (Whitfield, 1987); therefore, the characteristics discussed in this chapter may be typical of a broad spectrum of college students. Emotionally neglected students may present behavior problems on campus, act socially withdrawn, display obvious emotional difficulties, or exhibit exceptionally gifted social and academic talents. Within their home environments, emotional neglect may have been subtly expressed, or so blatantly expressed that the family colluded to guard it as a secret. Consequently, it is usually within counseling sessions with college students that the secrets of their emotionally neglectful homes and their hidden pain are revealed.

This chapter defines emotional neglect and its various forms, as described in recent literature. Although the most riveting experiences of emotional neglect usually occur during early childhood, the consequences extend through the college years and beyond. The visible and seemingly invisible signs of emotional neglect exhibited by college students are discussed and illustrated through case studies, to assist student services professionals in identifying students who may be silently crying for help. Finally, recommendations are made for providing help to college students from emotionally neglectful homes.

Defining Emotional Neglect

Succinctly defined, emotional neglect occurs when parents are "unable to provide necessary nurturance, stimulation, encouragement, and protection to a child at various stages of development, which inhibits his [or her] optimal functioning" (Garbarino, Guttmann, and Seeley, 1986, p. 2). Emotional neglect occurs as much in acts of omission as in acts of commission. In addition to blatant acts committed toward the child, emotional neglect can take the subtle form of deprivation, such as withholding affection from the child. Moreover, emotional neglect is not restricted to malicious intent on the part of the caregiver; it may result from a parent's physical and emotional illness or from economic constraints. It may even occur when a parent tries to be a better parent than he or she endured as a child.

According to Garbarino, Guttmann, and Seeley (1986), there are degrees in the severity of emotional neglect, which have varying consequences in an individual's life. For instance, mild neglect may lead to limited emotional difficulties, restricted to one aspect of development, such as shyness in social situations. Moderate neglect may impede the achievement of minimal success in significant settings, such as school. Severe neglect usually robs the individual of fulfillment in one or more of the major life functions—that is, work, love, or leisure. Popular theories of emotionally neglectful homes seem to focus either on the implications for the child as he or she currently resides in the home (for instance, "hurried children") or on the implications for the adult child (for instance, "prisoners of childhood").

Theories of Emotionally Neglected Children

Researchers and clinicians who have studied and observed the development of today's children have identified circumstances of emotional neglect as it occurs in the home. In each instance, the child internalizes the messages communicated by the parent's intentional or unintentional neglect. In response, the child usually overachieves or underachieves to compensate for his or her feelings of deprivation.

Latchkey Children. The term *latchkey children* refers to children who are regularly left unsupervised for some period of the day, typically before and/or after school (Long and Long, 1983). Such arrangements often occur when both parents (or, in single-parent households, the only parent) work during the hours when the child is home alone. The degree of severity of emotional neglect is influenced by the age of the child, the type of arrangements, the nature of the parent-child relationship, and the environmental context. Factors that diminish the degree of neglect experienced by the child include frequent telephone calls from the parent(s), positive relationships with the parent(s) and within the family system, a safe neighborhood that reduces realistic fears of being left alone, and opportunities to play outside or invite responsible friends to visit (Robinson, Rowland, and Coleman, 1986).

Studies suggest that both positive and negative outcomes occur in children from latchkey homes. Positive characteristics may include self-reliance and independence due to early responsibilities, effective self-help and prob-lem-solving skills, and increased maturity (Robinson, Rowland, and Cole-man, 1986). The risks, however, may include feelings of rejection or alienation, delinquency and vandalism, academic failure, accidents, and sexual victimization (Garbarino, 1984). Families with latchkey children are often in at least a minimal state of stress or crisis (Garbarino, 1984). Parents' conflicts between responsibilities to employers and financial need and responsibilities to children's needs for nurturing and attention may cause such stress. Children may internalize parental stress and blame themselves for creating the child-care dilemma. A child may become overly responsible, to ease the burden on his or her parents, or the child may act out to gain attention from the parents.

Hurried Children. Elkind (1981) argues that children in today's society are pressured to grow up too fast. They are expected to acquire the physical, psychological, and social attitudes and behaviors of adulthood well before they have the developmental abilities to deal with such aspects of life. Exam-ples of such practices of pushing children (usually "for their own good") into pseudomaturity include exerting pressure for children's early academic achievement (for instance, by enrolling them early in preschool), dressing them in adultlike clothing (such as designer clothes), entering them into orga-nized competitive sports (for instance, training for Olympic or professional sports), having them travel alone (such as on airline flights across the coun-try), and permitting their exposure, through music, television, movies, books, and magazines, to implicit and explicit sexual situations. The obvious pos-itive results of such hurrying are intelligent, well-groomed, highly trained, courageous, mature children who relieve their parents of the stresses of child-rearing (Long, 1984). Through all the pressures, however, the child may expe-rience stress from the fear of failure and the anxiety of not achieving fast enough or high enough. In addition, the child may become overly sensitive to the importance of coping, without feeling the confusion or pain of such premature developmental changes (Elkind, 1981). Elkind further warns of the risks of school failure, juvenile delinquency, drug abuse, suicide, chronic somatic conditions (such as headaches or stomachaches), chronic unhapp-iness, and hyperactive or lethargic behavior. The child may pay a heavy price for the parents' childrearing achievements.

Psychologically Battered Children. More severe cases of emotional neglect occur when parents psychologically batter their children through words and actions. Such abuse jeopardizes the development of self-esteem, social competence, the capacity for intimacy, and positive and healthy inter-personal relationships (Garbarino, Guttmann, and Seeley, 1986). Examples of verbal maltreatment include irritable scoldings and belittling comparisons with other children. Psychological maltreatment also includes threats of abandonment or loss, such as constant arguing between parents, changes from one mother figure to another, and periods of separation with strangers in unfamiliar places. Inconsistent and contradictory parental expectations and behaviors, restricted opportunities to play and socialize, and limited opportunities to be responsible and exercise critical thinking in problematic situations also impede the personal and social development of children. Mild, moderate, and severe forms of rejecting, terrorizing, ignoring, isolating, and corrupting all have effects on the psychological development of children. The consequences include hostile, aggressive, and destructive attitudes and behaviors; feelings of worthlessness, isolation, depression and anxiety; and such self-destructive behaviors as eating disorders and suicide attempts. Interpersonally, children may show excessive dependence on parents and other adults or defensively feigned independence. Again, some children respond through irresponsibility, while others respond through overresponsibility (Garbarino, Guttmann, and Seeley, 1986).

Regardless of the child's expressive reactions to emotional neglect, these patterns of personal belief and interpersonal interaction may remain a part of the individual into the college years. For instance, former latchkey children may harbor negative reactions to unresolved stress associated with too much responsibility at an early age (Long and Long, 1983), causing them to become severely overwhelmed when they are stressed by exams. Similarly, former hurried children may rush to experiment with their freedom in college, and the pressures they endured to grow up fast may collide with institutional rules of social behavior (Elkind, 1981). Former psychologically battered children may isolate themselves socially while in college or may join antisocial groups (Garbarino, Guttmann, and Seeley, 1986). Some students may thrive on competitive opportunities for achievement, while others may lose all their enthusiasm for school.

Mental health issues, such as depression, sleeping disturbances, migraine headaches associated with stress, drug and alcohol abuse, eating disorders, and suicidal ideation, may surface during the college years. Since these children's means of survival in the home was to mask their true feelings, however, they may continue to don masks of extreme capability on the college campus, and so mental health issues may be concealed. Once these children have left home to attend college, they may lose control of the overworked defenses that helped them cope and survive their emotionally neglectful homes.

A word of caution is needed in that the consequences of these forms of neglect cannot be generalized to all college students. Many factors influence a given individual's response to neglect, including ego strength, nurturing from extended family or other significant adults, and the cultural norms of the individual's ethnic group and/or socioeconomic level.

Theories of Emotionally Neglected Adult Children

Clinicians who have worked with countless adults from childhood homes exhibiting emotional neglect have observed patterns of characteristics that have shaped these individuals' lives into adulthood. Within their practices, these clinicians have journeyed back to infancy with their clients and explored the heartrending experiences of emotional deprivation and neglect that have been pervasive in their clients' lives. These life stories have provided deep insight into the hidden scars of emotionally neglected homes. A number of recent popular books (Forward, 1989; Miller, 1981; Shengold, 1989) exemplify the magnitude of the terror, constraint, and psychological damage internalized by adult children from emotionally neglectful homes.

Toxic Parents. Forward (1989, p. 6) chose the word *toxic* to describe the parents in her recent book because, "like a chemical toxin, the emotional damage inflicted by these parents spreads throughout a child's being and as the child grows, so does the pain." Examples of toxic parenting include leaving the child alone too much, inflicting continuous trauma and severe criticism, overprotecting or overburdening the child with guilt, and being severely depressed or unavailable because of emotional or physical illness. Forward has observed patterns of characteristics in adults who were victims of toxic parenting. These characteristics include damaged self-esteem, feelings of inadequacy, self-destructive behavior, perfectionism, difficulty relaxing and experiencing enjoyment, and lack of awareness of oneself or one's own needs. These feelings are associated with the fact that children of toxic parents tend to blame themselves for their parents' neglect because, as defenseless children, they could not accept the reality that their parents could not be trusted. Toxic parenting also tends to affect adult children's interpersonal relationships in that they repeatedly choose destructive or abusive relationships, feel mistrustful of others, and live with the constant fear of abandonment by significant others. These characteristics are likely to be seen during the college years. In the following case, a student presents a problem related to his academic goals, yet there are underlying problems that reflect his childhood defenses in surviving a toxic parenting situation:

> J. is a twenty-two-year-old Caucasian male. He is a senior, majoring in psychology, with a 3.8 grade-point average. J. entered counseling for assistance in deciding on graduate school. He applied to the top doctoral programs in psychology and is experiencing extreme anxiety because he fears that he may not get accepted to the program ranked number one in the country. J. is also experiencing difficulty in his romantic relationship. He has been dating the same young woman for two years, but he receives very little support from her when he needs it. He is clearly the caretaker in the relationship, yet he constantly fears that she will end it.
>
> During the counseling sessions, it was revealed that from the time J. was ten years old, his mother was in and out of the hospital because of major depression. His father worked very hard to maintain a family

atmosphere for J. and his younger brother and sister. J. took over many of the domestic responsibilities. His mother maintained a symbolic place in the family, but because of her periodic absences and her emotional unavailability, she could not provide a nurturing influence.

An initial indication of J.'s childhood with a toxic parent was his perfectionistic tendency and extreme anxiety, as exemplified by his insistence that he get accepted by the graduate program ranked number one in the country. His romantic relationship paralleled the caretaking role he had maintained in his family. There seemed to be no basis for his fear that his girl friend would end the relationship, which may indicate his fear of abandonment, based on his mother's physical and emotional abandonment.

Prisoners of Childhood. Miller (1981, p. 21) discovered through her clinical work with adults from emotionally neglectful homes that the "true self cannot communicate because it has remained . . . undeveloped in its inner prison." Children need parents who accept them fully and understand and support them. They need parents who allow them to openly express their feelings. Without such open relationships, children may fear that expressing unacceptable emotions will result in the loss of their parents' love. Consequently, such children fail to experience their true emotions. They become attuned to the needs and expectations of parents and develop acceptable personas, "false selves" devoid of any feelings of their own. They then live for the needs of their parents, which justifies their whole existence. Examples of parents who create these prisonlike relationships with their children include emotionally insecure parents who depend on a child's behavior to display their own self-images and parents who try to fulfill their own unmet childhood needs through their children: "If the child's demands become too great . . . [the parent] can bring the child up in such a way that he [or she] neither cries nor disturbs [the parent]" (Miller, 1981, p. 36). The child is encouraged to develop intellectual capacities but not emotional responses. Miller (1983) explains that as long as children are able to defend themselves by expressing the pain and anger of their suffering, they will overcome the damage caused by the neglect. If the parents cannot tolerate their children's reactions, whether crying, sadness, or rage, they will prevent their children from reacting in an individual way and will thus shape their children's silence.

College students who are "prisoners of childhood" are likely to be exceptional and gifted in every way. Their intellectual capacities were the only true expressions they were allowed to develop as children; consequently, they tend to be academically gifted. They may be involved in numerous extracurricular activities, given their sense of responsibility and their identities as caretakers. Nevertheless, whenever they are not "the star," or when they suddenly feel that they have failed to live up to some phenomenal self-image, they become anxious or develop feelings of guilt or shame. Even when they are admired and envied by others, they may carry depression, emptiness, and self-alienation inside themselves. According to Miller (1981, p. 21), they "are never overtaken by unexpected emotions, and will only admit those feelings that are accepted and approved by their inner censor, which is derived from their parent's heir." Socially, these college students may have an abundance of friends because they are so capable of empathizing with others. They may appear attentive, lively, and sensitive. If you were to discuss their childhoods and home lives with them, they would probably maintain the illusion of a good childhood, actually believing this themselves, since their denial is so strong; they are devoid of real emotional understanding of their childhood. The following case illustrates the disguised, visible signs of a student's childhood until her feelings of low self-esteem were assessed in a training workshop:

> T. is a twenty-year-old African-American female. She is a junior, majoring in engineering, with a 4.0 grade-point average. She is involved in a variety of extracurricular activities, including being resident assistant for the Office of Residential Living, tutoring, holding an office in the African-American Student Association, and participating in the student engineering club.
>
> T.'s feelings of low self-esteem surfaced recently during a Residential Living workshop for staff. T.'s supervisor observed that T.'s profile on a self-esteem inventory was very low particularly relative to the energetic image that T. constantly maintains. When questioned about her feelings of low self-esteem, T. denied that anything of an emotionally upsetting nature was going on in her life. It was only after several informal conversations with T. that her supervisor discovered that T.'s boyfriend had recently ended their three-year relationship. T. had not discussed the pain she was experiencing over this loss with anyone, because she believed this would be futile. She also feared that if she disclosed her pain to her father, he would be angry because he disapproved of her having a boyfriend, nor did she turn to her mother for support, because T. feared that her mother would be hurt: it would remind her of the pain she had suffered in her relationship with T.'s father.

Soul Murder. Shengold (1989) has poignantly described the emotional crimes of commission and omission against children as "soul murder": "Murdering someone's soul means depriving the victim of the ability to feel joy and love as a separate person" (Shengold, 1989, p. 2). Shengold tells of his clinical work with adults from homes in which "love and empathy are described as never or only intermittently present—cold indifference or destructive hatred reigns. Often one hears of a kind of brainwashing, a cultivation of denial by the parents that makes the child doubt the evidence of his or her own senses and memory" (Shengold, 1989, pp. 14–15). Soul murder is the deliberate attempt by parents to annihilate or distort the separate identity of a child. Parents treat their children as if they were extensions of themselves or objects to satisfy their own desires. Since children are dependent for their physical and emotional needs, they have no choice but to submit and identify with their abusive parents. Such torture and deprivation, coupled with complete dependency, elicit overwhelming feelings of helplessness and rage, but these feelings must be suppressed for the children to survive in their homes. Eventually, the continual retreat from these feelings compromises even positive emotions, and these children are ultimately robbed of all feeling.

College students may displace their long-denied hostility onto others, or they may internalize their parents' punitiveness and develop a need for self-punishment. They may set themselves up for failure academically, socially, or in love relationships, to ensure that they will be ridiculed and punished by others, as they believe they deserve. The devastating consequences of soul murder may be psychotic, psychopathic, or criminal behavior (Shengold, 1989). In contrast, some students may have contained the terrifying effects so tightly that there will be no visible signs of their tormented pasts. According to Shengold (1989, p. 6), they may function "as if they are psychologically healthy, presenting a façade of normality that covers an essential hollowness of soul." Some students actually develop adaptive qualities (such as negotiating, taking care of others, pretending, or denying), which assisted them in merely surviving in their home environments but serve them exceptionally well in the comparatively tame environments of the college campus. The following case portrays a student who is naturally capable of progressing successfully through college, but her extreme identification with her mother may lead to self-destructive behaviors that may thwart her:

> B. is an eighteen-year-old Hispanic female. She is in her second semester of college, on a full premed scholarship. She is a peer counselor for one of the supportive services programs. B. is very attractive and has a vibrant personality. She frequently stops by to talk informally with Ms. Brooks, the peer-counselor coordinator. Ms. Brooks has noticed that B. seems to go through some personal crisis during midterms and finals each semester. She has also recently heard rumors that B. has developed a reputation for sexual permissiveness.
>
> Given Ms. Brooks's relationship with B., she felt that she could inquire about B.'s romantic relationships. B. used this opportunity to pour her heart out about each of the five young men with whom she had been hopelessly in love since college began. Each one stopped seeing her, usually around exam time, shortly after she had become sexually involved with him. B. was optimistic, however, that her new boyfriend

really loved her, and that she would finally show her mother that a boy could love her for herself and not just for her body.

B. revealed that her father had abandoned her and her mother when she was an infant. B.'s mother has not had a steady relationship with a man since that time and she constantly admonishes B. that neither of them will ever be able to trust a man. B. represents an example of a "soul murder" victim in that her mother brainwashed her into believing that she was doomed to failed relationships with men. Consequently, B. engaged in misguided efforts to prove her mother wrong, but her efforts ultimately fulfilled her mother's prophecy.

These theoretical perspectives and case studies seem to involve extreme cases of emotional neglect, but they do reflect relatively common clinical experiences with adults and college students who survived and found a safe place to tell their stories. Their willingness to share and relive the secrets of their pasts with professional therapists has been the key to knowledge and understanding, which in turn has opened the doors to the healing process for survivors of emotionally neglectful homes. Case studies have revealed that the longer an individual lives in the silence of his or her neglected childhood, the more disruptive the events of the past can be to present and future functioning.

Recommendations for Campus Responses

In light of the pervasive nature and the various forms of emotional neglect described in this chapter, student services staff may feel perplexed about how they can make a difference to a college student who has experienced emotional neglect. Essentially, the unmet needs for love and attention remain with the individual; regardless of age, the individual's needs can be met whenever he or she encounters a supportive relationship. Consequently, anyone in a campus environment may be in the position of providing help to a student from an emotionally neglectful home. In fact, the student who is currently a roommate, best friend, classmate, pupil, student worker, resident assistant, peer counselor, tutor, fraternity brother or sorority sister, or student government president may be one of the walking, talking wounded.

Attend to the Hidden Messages. Anyone involved in a relationship with a survivor of an emotionally neglectful home must understand the contradiction between the external behaviors and the internal feelings of such a student. These students have carefully created their worlds of continuous displays of gratitude to their parents for "all that they have given them." They may be perceived as born leaders because of their keen sense of responsibility, but the leaders in them were created in the psyches of these neglected children; they are roles played out time and again in their dreams and fantasies.

The affection and applause that they win with their outstanding accomplishments and charming dispositions are attempts to compensate for missing the kind word, the tender touch, the gentle smile that was their unpaid due just for being their parents' children. Yet the applause will never be enough, for by now they have been conditioned to believe that they have just done what they were supposed to do; thus, acceptance of the rewards would seem fraudulent to them. Interestingly enough, the skills that they are praised for mastering so exceptionally represent mere exercises in survival for them, since these were the interpersonal behaviors and intrapsychic dynamics that allowed them to live through the neglect of days gone by. While they are cheered in the public eye, they are denied the private pleasures and unconditional rewards of personal worth, peace of mind, and intimate loving relationships.

According to Whitfield (1987), emotionally neglected students may conceal their true feelings through masks of shame, such as anger, blame, control, perfectionism, or compulsive behavior. Their compulsive behaviors, such as alcohol and drug use, short-term intense relationships, attempts to control others, eating disorders, sexual addiction, overworking, or overspending, may be attempts at relief from feelings of tension, numbness, and pain, They hope to feel alive again, if only for a brief time, but end up feeling shameful and incomplete later. Their nonverbal behaviors (hanging the head, slumped shoulders, avoidance of eye contact, nervous laughter, constant apologies for having needs and rights) may be visible clues to their shame.

Initiate Discussions of Home Life. College students often experience being away from home as an opportunity to begin sharing stories of their family life. Expressing and sorting out their true feelings about childhood represents the beginning stages of developing autonomy. If you suspect that a student comes from a troubled past, use the relationship with that student to engage him or her in conversations about families. Beginning with the subtle demographics of family composition (number of siblings, parents' occupations) is relatively safe for the student. Anecdotal tales of childhood experiences at home can be shared as the relationship deepens.

The college campus is a likely place for healing to begin. No matter what role an individual plays in an emotionally neglected student's life, that person can provide what the student needs most: a genuine relationship of acceptance and support, an ear to listen. A strong, trusting relationship is the cornerstone of the healing process, the foundation from which the student may begin to tell his or her story.

There are no prescribed ways in which students will share the stories of their past with individuals in the campus environment. Some students may laughingly describe seemingly painful episodes of their home life; such inappropriate affective expression typically indicates denial of genuine feelings. Other students may be reluctant to disclose information regarding their families. Such discomfort in disclosing family matters may be indicative of various factors, such as insufficient rapport in the relationship, an attempt to conceal the secrets of a dysfunctional family, or major cultural differences in the relationship. Helping relationships require time for the individuals involved to feel comfortable in trusting each other.

Refer for Professional Help. Student services staff must assess the level of students' functioning and the severity of the stories they reveal, to determine whether a referral is necessary. Some students from mildly neglectful homes may not require professional counseling; they may need only the continued support of nurturing adults who allow them to be their true selves. Other students, however, have no awareness of their true feelings and life perceptions, and it is necessary to refer them for professional help.

In referring students for therapy, it is crucial for the students to feel that their relationships with the referring persons will continue. Initially, student services staff and faculty serve as the bridges connecting students with professional therapists. In some cases, it may be necessary for staff to diminish students' dependence on them, so as not to impede the therapy process, but staff can assist by continuing to maintain supportive relationships. As students work through painful past experiences in therapy, they will need nurturing relationships in the campus environment for encouragement and comfort.

Often the referral source feels left in the dark once he or she has referred a student to a counseling center; issues of confidentiality prevent therapists from keeping the referring persons abreast of students' progress. Therefore, it is helpful for staff and students to understand what students may experience as they enter therapy. Whitfield (1987) has described stages for recovering from dysfunctional families that provide a framework for helping staff and students better understand the therapy process.

The Healing Process. The healing process begins when students recognize that the ways of relating to themselves and others may be leftover survival skills that are ineffective in the college environment—for instance, being the loyal listener to all of their friends' problems, but never being able to disclose their own problems. Such quasi-intimacy is common practice among students from emotionally neglectful homes.

Difficulty in mastering the developmental tasks of young adulthood often triggers in students the feeling that their childhoods were not what they seemed to be. They may experience confusion, fear, sadness, numbness, anger, or excitement and enthusiasm (Whitfield, 1987). Developmental tasks such as (1) struggling with the change from dependence on parents to independence, (2) dealing with authority, (3) learning to deal with uncertainty, ambiguity, and confusing emotions such as love and hate, (4) developing a mature sexuality, (5) finding security and developing a sense of self-competence, and (6) developing their own standards and value systems (Farnsworth, 1966) all have an emotional foundation that may consist of damaging messages that were internalized during childhood. Additional triggers of discord may include involvement in intimate relationships, confronting major life transitions, experiencing performance demands, and particularly, making visits home to their parents (Whitfield, 1987).

The first two stages, survival of the past and awakening to the reality of the past, may be as far as students can reach on their own. The next stage, finding help, may occur accidentally as they turn to the closest available person; or they may consciously choose a safe, informative relationship or group in which to begin to explore the past.

As students begin to deal with the past, they must confront such core issues as: (1) needing total control, (2) being over-responsible, (3) neglecting their own needs, (4) tolerating highly inappropriate behavior, based on their childhood experiences of "normal" behavior, and (5) fearing abandonment, which is expressed in their mistrust of and withdrawal from others (Whitfield, 1987).

Another major issue is students' difficulty handling and resolving conflict. Often students will either withdraw from situations of conflict or become aggressive in an attempt to overpower the source of contention (Whitfield, 1987). The college environment provides many opportunities for teaching students how to handle conflict. First, they must recognize that they are in a situation of dissonance, as many students find themselves reacting with no awareness of what is going on. Basically, they are responding unconsciously to early memories of childhood conflict, and their reactions are usually out of proportion to the present conflict. After students learn to recognize conflict, they must be encouraged to take the risk of conveying their concerns, feelings, and needs in the situation. This is a particularly difficult step for students from neglectful homes because they have been socialized to ignore their true emotions and deny their own needs.

The next stage, beginning to talk about the past, may go on indefinitely. Most students who have denied and repressed their painful past are not aware themselves of the whole story. Therefore, the most important aspect of this stage is for them to uncover the truth themselves. Students must tell their stories and express their feelings at their own pace, so as not to trigger childhood defense mechanisms. They may cry during one session and be so frightened by their own expression of feeling that they laugh about their childhood during the next session.

The process of telling their stories initiates the grieving process, which is the final stage of letting go of the past. Students must relive their feelings and experiences in the comfort of a safe and supportive relationship in order to get in touch with the sorrow, despair, anger, and rage over the neglect and deprivation they suffered as children. During this stage, they may actually feel as though they are living interchangeably in the past and the present. As students move through the grieving process, they will gradually become more and more in touch with their true selves and experience being real for the first time.

Additional Campus Interventions. Psychoeducational and support group interventions for survivors of emotional neglect should become a regular part of the programming efforts on college campuses. Through psychoeducational interventions in the residence halls, the classrooms, the counseling center, and various offices in student services, students will feel that their childhood experiences have been validated as real-life events. Consequently, they will become open to exploring the past and become less fearful of the horror they may discover. If exploration of oneself and one's family background is perceived as a normal part of the growth process in the college years, then it may prevent the development of serious self-destructive alternatives as attempts to conceal the past. In addition, mentoring programs with faculty and staff provide opportunities for developing significant relationships with caring adults. Such relationships can facilitate a corrective experience for students in that mentors can substitute care and concern where there once was parental neglect.

This chapter has attempted to help student services staff become aware of quietly problematic students, who were neglected as children and who, perhaps because of their exceptional coping skills, may be inadvertently neglected in the campus environment. Theoretical examples of some forms of childhood neglect, and case studies of students who are survivors of emotional neglect, were provided to clarify the nature of the problem. Finally, recommendations were made for campus responses to students from emotionally neglectful homes. In conclusion, to walk with a student through the sorrow and pain of the past and to nurture him or her along the journey is a mutual gift for the student and the helper. The helper gives the gift of love, and the student gives the gift of trust.

References

Elkind, D. *The Hurried Child.* Reading, Mass.: Addison-Wesley, 1981.

Farnsworth, D. L. *Psychiatry, Education, and the Young Adult.* Springfield, Ill.: Thomas, 1966.

Forward, S. *Toxic Parents.* New York: Bantam Books, 1989.

Garbarino, J. "Can American Families Afford the Luxury of Childhood?" Unpublished manuscript, Pennsylvania State University, 1984.

Garbarino, J., Guttmann, E., Seeley, J. *The Psychologically Battered Child: Strategies for Identification, Assessment, and Intervention.* San Francisco: Jossey-Bass, 1986.

Long, T. "So Who Cares If I'm Home?" *Educational Horizons,* 1984, 62, 60–64.

Long, T. J., and Long, L. *The Handbook of Latchkey Children and Their Parents.* New York: Arbor House, 1983.

Miller, A. *Prisoners of Childhood.* New York: Basic Books, 1981.

Miller, A. *For Your Own Good.* New York: Farrar Straus Giroux, 1983.

Robinson, B., Rowland, B., and Coleman, M. *Latchkey Kids.* Lexington, Mass.: Heath, 1986.

Shengold, L. *Soul Murder.* New Haven, Conn.: Yale University Press, 1989.

Whitfield, C. L. *Healing the Child Within.* Deerfield Beach, Fla.: Health Communications, 1987.

Donelda A. Cook is an assistant professor in the Department of Counseling and Personnel Services at the University of Maryland, College Park.

This chapter discusses the issues and implications of higher education's responses to the concerns of students from dysfunctional backgrounds.

Student Affairs Administrators React

Fred B. Newton, Robert S. Krause

In reading the chapters of this volume, it becomes apparent that any discussion of the background development of students encompasses a vast realm of possibilities. The college environment is very much a melting pot of society and, as such, the family backgrounds of its students vary widely and in many ways reflect the general population. In simplest terms, the focus of concern is about the impact of nurture, especially negative background experience, on people and how it may affect a student's present college life. The issues of dysfunction, in this context, become especially relevant to those in student affairs positions who have embraced the model of student development as a raison d'être in the educational arena, to support the total growth of the individual in social, emotional, physical, and personal ways, as well as intellectual. A question arises: If students' development is thwarted or retarded, is there not some obligation to understand why and help the student overcome these obstacles and achieve higher levels of potential?

The debate concerning how much responsibility an education environment assumes for the personal and social development of an individual has continued from the days of *in loco parentis*. How much and what type of involvement should student affairs staff have in the lives of students? Furthermore, there are questions of priority, in which the needs of social responsibility are balanced by the practical considerations of budget constraint. Student affairs administrators must make choices to implement the kinds of programs and services that assist the educational mission. At the same time, they must be careful not to get caught up in trendy decisions that create another brief niche of specialization. The purpose of this chapter is to consider the impacts of family dysfunction on college students and how student service departments and divisions can respond.

NEW DIRECTIONS FOR STUDENT SERVICES, no. 54, Summer 1991 © Jossey-Bass Inc., Publishers

The various points made in the previous chapters are organized here through five observations. We identify some of the issues that confront the practitioner and administrator and discuss some of the options for institutional response. In some cases, the need for further research and clarification is noted, since there is obviously much to be learned and determined in overcoming the problems of dysfunction with individuals, family systems, and society in general. We believe that the most successful institutional responses to these problems will come from assessment of existing campus and community resources and discussion of the information presented in the preceding chapters. In short, there are no quick, "cookbook" approaches. What follows is presented for inclusion in campus discussions. Ultimately, the chief student affairs officer and professional staff on each campus are responsible for developing and implementing appropriate responses to students' needs.

1. *The experience of dysfunction in the family of origin is a ubiquitous phenomenon that potentially is a concern if not an influence for the majority of college students.* A few statistics reported in the preceding chapters illustrate this point. In the next decade, over 50 percent of college-age youth will have experienced their parents' divorce; 10 to 20 percent of present college students have witnessed family violence; nearly 25 percent of the population has at least one parent with a drinking problem; a quarter or more of all women have been victims of sexual abuse; and as many as 80 percent of all children have been neglected (for example, by having to be at home by themselves at an early age).

The pervasiveness of problems in the family or nurturing environment during the important developmental years leads to several possible conceptualizations. The most apparent one is that of an *epidemic.* The "epidemic" perception justifies mobilizing increased efforts in society (in this case, the college or university campus) to remedy or counteract potential negative consequences. Another possible conceptualization would follow a *sociological* point of view, which says that the data reflect the decline of the traditional American family and, with that decline, a decay of important functions for the protection, nurturance, and development of children. The sociological view might then suggest a return to the promotion of those family values, or a discovery of alternative social systems that can replace, supplement, or redefine an appropriate childrearing process. Still another view would take a rather *existential* position. Peck (1978) expresses this stance with the phrase "life is difficult." He says that it is through an understanding and acceptance of this difficulty that people learn to cope, adjust, appreciate, and succeed in life. From this standpoint, it may be less important to dwell on the causal factors of one's position (for example, being a victim of the past) than to focus on the attitude or perspective for managing life by accepting one's present situation and assuming responsibility for more personal control and future direction.

It would seem important, before determining a response to the prevalence observation, to consider the validity of the viewpoints on which a
conclusion is reached. The three positions just described are examples of
how different perspectives can become basic tenets for interpreting a phenomenon and become pivotal underpinnings for the direction of a
response. Some discussion to consider differing viewpoints, such as debat-
ing the difference between sociological and individual interpretations, or
between sickness and wellness perspectives, would be a provocative backdrop for addressing the concern of family dysfunction and its implications
for student development.

2. *We need more data.* It is difficult to determine whether the perceived
increase in reported abuse or other dysfunction during the past decade is
a result of actual increases or of a more aware and open stance than in the
past. Another explanation is that researchers and practitioners themselves
may now be asking questions about abuse and dysfunction that were not
asked a few years ago. Additional data could also help clarify the interre-
latedness of dysfunctions. For example, it is known that there is a strong
degree of association between alcohol use and sexual abuse or spouse
assault. Comparisons of dysfunctional patterns would help us understand
problems and, perhaps, better discern relationships among family, economic, hereditary, and other factors.

The preceding chapters constitute a primer of information, which
should be included in the curriculum of all college student personnel and
higher education preparation programs. Campus surveys or other data-
gathering methods would be helpful in determining the extent of problems
in the environment. In-service professional development programs on campuses should also make this information available to student affairs practitioners. Further research, exploring dysfunctional experiences and abusive
experiences in relationship to students' inability to accomplish developmental tasks, is warranted.

3. *Dysfunctions in the backgrounds of students may be identified through
discernible symptoms, which interfere with the achievement of successful development whether in relationships, academic accomplishment, emotional maturity,
career direction, or personal happiness.* It is suggested that surveys, or other
problem-identification methods, be used as a way to assess, diagnose, and
define the nature of the individual situation and determine the breadth of
the problem across the campus. A number of available checklists may be
helpful in a systematic assessment approach, particularly with the concerns
of ACOAs and alcohol and drug use. Very few of these, however, have
become standardized instruments with well-established normative data.

It would also be important to assess these symptoms on a number of
other dimensions, which may serve better to delimit areas of concern.
Level of severity, with emphasis on current functioning, is one dimension
that seems helpful to determine. Stress levels and emotional reactions can

be identified, to provide some description of the nature of one's response and functional status. From a developmental perspective, there are now instruments, based on report of task achievement and characteristics of the individual, that describe developmental levels and can elucidate the stage or task that is predominant with an individual. Of course, all instruments are only as good as the accuracy of measuring a concept, and consideration must be given to the instruments' reliability and validity. The practitioner must determine what is to be assessed and the type of instrument or process that is available to make such an assessment. Table 1 outlines some of the symptoms described in the preceding chapters. As intervention strategies are developed with this type of checklist, probable antecedent conditions could also be listed and compared to those actually experienced by students exhibiting symptoms. In this way, relationships between symptoms and antecedent conditions may be clarified.

One issue presented by this approach to intervention is the emphasis that it puts on illness. Intervention occurs in this model when something is identified as wrong, and a person seeks assistance to remedy the deficiency. Are there other ways to intervene that could emphasize prevention or education? One important element to balance the deficiency approach would be the inclusion of information about people with hearty or adaptive personalities. These are people who have experienced family dysfunction but have adjusted well and may have even benefited from mastering an early crisis of development. What is it that distinguishes these people? Would we not learn valuable information by looking at the process of adjustment with the highly functioning individual?

The student development model has been described as both a theoretical position and a process model for understanding how students go through various tasks of growth on several key dimensions. Chickering (1972) identifies several of these key tasks as gaining autonomy, clarifying purpose, achieving competence, establishing identity, developing integrity, stabilizing emotions, and freeing interpersonal relationships. Creamer (1980), Miller and Prince (1976), and Newton and Ender (1980) have described how student development can be implemented in higher education through intentional process. These approaches have emphasized the use of assessment, awareness enhancement, and intervention through strategies in the living environment, classroom, or extracurricular activities of students that may positively facilitate their growth. Individuals may be fixed or stuck at certain levels on specific dimensions in their development. Through assessment and appropriate intervention, they can work through and move on to progress to accumulatively higher levels of task accomplishment, whether identifying their purpose in life or freeing interpersonal relationships. Another theoretical model, which would seem important to understand clearly and use in working with students from dysfunctional backgrounds, is the family and social systems model. Caple (1987) and

Table 1. Characteristic Symptoms of Students
from Dysfunctional Backgrounds

Symptom Area	Symptom	Brief Description
Affective	Stress reactions	Excessive anxiety, physiological stress conditions (stomachaches, headaches, somatic disorders), worry and obsessive rumination
	Anger control	Inappropriate ventilation of anger and frustration, pent-up or repressed hostility
	Withdrawal	Distancing, denial, and other avoidance of feelings
	Depression	Biological change in sleep, eating, appearance; lethargy, low activity; self-deprecation/alienation
	Fear	Incapacity to decide or act, social phobias
	Emotional pain (grief)	Unresolved reactions to loss easily provoked (may contain many elements of grief stages)
Self-Concept	Negativity/ pessimism	Pervasive sense of doom or despair about life
	Personal ambivalence	Uncertainty; confusion about personal interest, ability, identity
	Seeing self as different	Embarrassment; feeling inferior to others
	Overachievement	Continually striving to prove oneself to others
	Being over-controlled (or undercontrolled)	Lack of spontaneity; acting out without consideration of consequences
Social	Excessive caretaking	Overresponsibility or dependence in significant relationship
	Conflict	Continual fighting and unresolved disputes; dissension, abuse
	Manipulation	Using indirect means to elicit responses and acquire desired attention (or other outcome); may involve lying and coverups
	Repetitive patterns	Repeating and recreating dysfunctional patterns in new relationships
Addictive	Alcohol or drug use	Chronic and dysfunctional alcohol and/or drug use to carry out work, school, or social obligations
	Love	Confusing love and need; destructive interactions; repetitive but unsatisfying relationships

Durkin (1981) have described the principles that operate in an ever changing exchange and interchange between the boundaries of self and others in a world that is social in context. It is crucial to understand how the interaction of multiple influences and group interactions will collectively and dynamically influence individual behavior.

4. *The intervention strategies cited in the preceding chapters make use of a broad continuum of services and strategies already employed by campuses to help students accomplish developmental tasks more successfully.* Table 2 presents a list of responses that have been suggested throughout the chapters of this volume. These responses are not meant to be inclusive, nor are they rec-

ommended for every setting, but they may serve as a checklist of possibilities that an institution would consider.

Selection of strategies or support services should take place after assessment of existing resources and after thorough discussion of the impacts of dysfunctional and/or abusive experiences on students' ability to accomplish developmental tasks. Some selections may be made with greater ease than others. For example, if assessment data at a campus reveal that students who have been sexually abused as children are experiencing difficulty in developing healthy dating relationships, a support group to share experiences and feelings about dating may be an appropriate campus response. It may be more difficult to determine the appropriate institutional response to the research that suggests that victims of childhood sexual abuse experience a greater frequency of alcoholism and drug addiction than do nonvictims. Are drug and alcohol treatment programs specifically for victims of childhood sexual abuse warranted? Should special efforts be made to screen students in existing drug or alcohol treatment groups to determine whether they have experienced childhood sexual abuse? As future research further

Table 2. Continuum of Suggested Interventions on Campus for Students from Dysfunctional Backgrounds

Category	Intervention	Example
Assessment	Campuswide surveys	Drug and alcohol behaviors
	Individual life-style assessments	Life-style and assessment questions
	Health histories	
	Checklists or inventories	
Education/ prevention	Orientation programs	Summer enrollment
	Campus radio/TV spots	
	Student newspapers	Articles/advertisements
	Educational presentations to campus groups	
	Wellness weeks	
	Campuswide task force	
	Train peer counselors/RAs	Peer programs
	Guest speakers	
	Assignment of responsibility to unit/agency	Coordinating agency
Support	Self-help groups	ACOA group
	Shelters	Crisis centers
	Referrals within community	Treatment programs
	Student conduct codes	Sexual assault standards
	Financial assistance	Emergency loans
	Administrative enforcement	Probation/suspension
	Ombudsperson	Negotiation/mediation
Treatment	Individual counseling	
	Family intervention	
	Group therapy	
Self Development	Self-defense classes	
	Skill-building workshops	Assertiveness training

clarifies the relationship between dysfunctional and abusive backgrounds and students' developmental tasks, strategies for intervention and development of support services will be refined.

5. *Individual service providers must adhere to the ethical standards and legal requirements prescribed by state law, community standards, institutional mission, and professional ethics or standards.* In many ways, the first four observations must be refined into a viable institutional response that carefully weighs the ethical, legal, and moral responsibilities of each situation. A few questions are raised as examples of this type of institutional process.

Are institutional procedures consistent with state and local statutes? For example, there may be laws that require reporting of abuse, felonies, or even threats of illegal activity. These laws may apply differently to various disciplines, according to the authority or certain communication privileges granted to state-licensed disciplines (medicine, law, psychology, counseling, social work). Are student service staff familiar with state requirements? If so, what would be the reporting structure for disclosing an identified problem? Furthermore, such standards of practice as confidentiality may seem at times to be in conflict with reporting requirements and the judgment of authenticity, as in the case of an allegation concerning abuse. How do staff consult and determine an appropriate yet legal response? Legal adherence, professional responsibility, and student welfare may be a complex set of issues necessitating an informed professional staff, a forum for clarification of the issues, and procedures that are applied consistently.

The philosophy and mission of an institution may also be called into question in determining a campus response. The 1960s were a period when most colleges and universities moved away from a position of parental responsibility, in the name of democratization. The next decade was often characterized as a time when students could "do their own thing," as individualization tended to lead in some situations to a lack of social responsibility. The more recent move has been to initiate more definitive standards for campus behavior and not to condone those behaviors that have negative social consequences. Examples are increased restrictions on drinking, whether requirements of age or an organizational mandate to have nonalcoholic beverages as alternatives at all sanctioned functions. Another example is procedures for reporting sexual assault and harassment that may not be prosecutable through the courts. Colleges are also starting to review the scope of their responsibility in serving as an alternative to changes in the family and social system. The presence of many single-parent students on campus has led to the initiation of day-care centers, with students sharing in contact and responsibility but also having support for the maintenance of their children. In a very real sense, higher education has had to consider ways in which the campus can help prevent the occurrence of abuse, neglect, or other dysfunctions for the next generation. The possibilities for the future will obviously extend even further. How can institutions consider their role and responsibility in meeting the needs of student and society and providing alternatives for their future?

As administrators, we believe that issues facing today's students that are a result of dysfunctions in background are indeed of serious concern to the campus community and must be addressed through the resources and activities of student service personnel. Promotion of understanding and increased knowledge of the problem and possible solutions can be accomplished through staff development. Each campus must be prepared to determine its manner of response, through the consideration of cooperative efforts and assigned responsibilities to specific agencies. Policies and procedures for promoting a healthy environment and curbing practices that continue dysfunctional patterns must be considered from a campuswide perspective. Further research and knowledge about the occurrence of dysfunction and its impact on individual performance must be promoted, so that effective treatment and prevention can be offered.

References

Caple, R. B. "The Change Process in Developmental Theory: A Self-Organization Paradigm, Part I." *Journal of College Student Development,* 1987, *28* (1), 4–11.

Chickering, A. W. *Education and Identity.* San Francisco: Jossey-Bass, 1972.

Creamer, D. G. (ed.). *Student Development in Higher Education.* Alexandria, Va.: American College Personnel Association, 1980.

Durkin, J. E. *Living Groups: Group Psychotherapy and General Systems Theory.* New York: Brunner/Mazel, 1981.

Miller, T. K., and Prince, J. S. *The Future of Student Affairs.* San Francisco: Jossey-Bass, 1976.

Newton, F. B., and Ender, K. L. *Student Development Practices: Strategies for Making a Difference.* Springfield, Ill.: Thomas, 1980.

Peck, M. S. *The Road Less Traveled.* New York: Simon & Schuster, 1978.

Fred B. Newton is director of University Counseling Services and associate professor of education at Kansas State University.

Robert S. Krause is vice-president for institutional advancement at Kansas State University. In this capacity, he serves as chief student affairs officer, as well as chief spokesperson for the institution.

CONCLUSION AND ADDITIONAL SOURCES

Editing this volume has been an exciting and rewarding experience. The contributors have collaborated to produce a single resource on how dysfunctional families can affect college students and what services college campuses can offer students from dysfunctional backgrounds. It is clear that families fall on a continuum from well functioning to severely dysfunctional, and college students come from a full range of backgrounds.

The contributors have offered significant evidence to support the position that students' psychological and behavioral disturbances often stem from dysfunctional family backgrounds. For instance, survivors of sexual abuse may be more vulnerable to incidents of coercive sex, students exposed to physical violence between their parents may become involved in violent dating relationships, and students from chemically impaired families may experience their own difficulties with alcohol or other drugs or may become involved in relationships with others who abuse chemicals. It is critical to avoid drawing the conclusion that a child who grows up in a dysfunctional family will lead a problematic life. Many people raised in dysfunctional families become healthy, independent, well-functioning adults. Many persons who have grown up in alcoholic families do not abuse alcohol as adults. Many survivors of sexual abuse do not abuse their own children or others.

According to Peele (1989, p. 278), "Even people from very precarious family and social backgrounds show the ability to rebound from all sorts of trauma. Human recuperative power is a remarkable thing." Peele speaks against labeling and interacting with people according to their problems—problems that more often than not, they will outgrow. Identifying college students as products of dysfunctional families can be helpful to students and campus professionals, but this identification process can be risky if we use family dysfunction as an excuse for or a denial of students' current emotional and behavioral problems. Another risk occurs when we label someone as an adult child of an alcoholic (ACOA) because he or she grew up in an alcoholic home. A colleague of mine whose father was an alcoholic recently shared her experience of reading literature on ACOAs. When she reviewed the personality and behavioral characteristics expected of ACOAs, she was able to identify with only a few of these qualities; she rejected the others. Many people, particularly young adults who have not gained a healthy level of self-awareness and self-confidence, may not be able to reject those characteristics often assigned to ACOAs. As a result, they may underestimate their personal strengths and capacities.

In a recent discussion with a client, the subject of this volume came up, since she is an entering freshman at a nearby college. After I described the purpose of this volume and listed each of the types of dysfunctional families, she said that her family had experienced two divorces, that her father has been an alcoholic for many years, that there was violence between her biological parents, and that she was sexually abused by a stepfather. She also described feeling emotionally neglected by her family. The odds are clearly against someone's growing up in a family that exhibits all the dysfunctional systems described in this volume. The client and I reviewed the progress she had made during counseling and discussed how confident she felt about starting college and moving on to the next phase of her life. She serves as an excellent example of someone who has demonstrated recuperative power and managed to acquire healthier life skills. This client is aware of the dysfunctional qualities in her family background and, for the most part, of how she has been affected. Labeling her as a "child of a dysfunctional family system" may only interfere with her journey toward psychological health.

A conclusion can be drawn that families have a powerful impact on children and continue to serve as a significant factor through late adolescence and young adulthood. When young people leave home to attend college, they may experience specific challenges, and students from dysfunctional families may experience additional demands. For example, unhealthy families usually do not encourage individuality and independence. When a student begins college, the family may be threatened by the idea of the student's becoming independent and may respond in an unsupportive manner or attempt to interfere. The entering freshman may have served a specific purpose in the family, and his or her absence may cause a crisis. Moreover, families that have had control over their children are no longer able to maintain as much control. Families with such secrets as incest, alcoholism, or violence can no longer be assured that these secrets will remain in the family. Dysfunctional families may continue to have negative effects on students, whether the students live at or away from home.

For example, a freshman from out of state was referred to the counseling center as a result of her suicide attempt. During the assessment process, she described how her father had sexually abused her and her sisters over a long period of time. The assessment resulted in a recommendation for her hospitalization. The student agreed with the recommendation and decided to enter a hospital more than three hundred miles from her family, since she was aware that she had revealed a family secret. She informed her brother of her decision and told him not to contact their parents. Within a few minutes, her father telephoned the counseling center and asked to speak to his daughter. He said that he and his wife were coming to campus, and that his daughter should not leave until they arrived. During a meeting with the parents, the father asked his daughter and his wife to leave the room. He said that his daughter often lied, and he wanted to know if she had told any unusual stories about the family. He decided to take her home. The student left only after her father promised to bring her to the hospital that had agreed to admit her for treatment. The parents broke this contract by admitting her to a hospital close to home and involving a psychiatrist who was an acquaintance of the father. After the student was released from the hospital and had returned to campus, she said that she could not reveal the incidents of sexual abuse, because her father's presence was too threatening. In a later discussion with her psychiatrist, it was also learned that neither the student nor her parents had disclosed her suicide attempt to the hospital staff; the only information provided was that she had been depressed. This example illustrates the level of threat experienced by dysfunctional parents when their children attempt to separate from them, and the extent to which these parents continue influencing their adult children's lives.

This example, as well as those presented throughout this volume, illustrates the challenges faced by universities in working with students from dysfunctional families. Each contributor to this volume recommends that we increase our understanding of students from dysfunctional families and provide developmental services consistent with the educational mission. Peele (1989) contends that we need to create genuine communities that nurture the human capacity to lead a constructive life. His message is very relevant to students from dysfunctional families and very valuable to the entire university community.

This section is for the reader who wants more information about dysfunctional families. It is not intended to be all-encompassing. Rather, it offers some current and valuable resources.

Children from Alcoholic Families

Middleton-Moz, J., and Dwinell, L. *After the Tears: Reclaiming the Personal Losses of Childhood.* Deerfield Beach, Fla.: Health Communications, 1986.

Establishes psychological understandings and treatment directions for adult children of alcoholics. The book is helpful not only for ACOAs but also for anyone from a dysfunctional family.

Utain, M., and Oliver B. *Scream Louder: Through Hell and Healing with an Incest Survivor and Her Therapist.* Deerfield Beach, Fla.: Health Communications, 1989.

Tells the story of one woman's painful journey through recovery from incest and family alcoholism. Provides steps for adults who grew up in dysfunctional families.

Child Sexual Abuse

Blume, E. S. *Secret Survivors: Uncovering Incest and Its Aftereffects in Women.* New York: Wiley, 1990.

Expands the definition of incest to include sexual abuse perpetrated by any caregiver, including teachers, doctors, and so forth. Focuses on the impacts of incest. Includes an incest survivor's aftereffects checklist.

Davis, L. *The Courage to Heal Workbook: For Women and Men Survivors of Child Sexual Abuse.* New York: Harper & Row, 1990.

This book extends the value of *The Courage to Heal* (Bass and Davis, 1988) by translating the stages of the healing process into practical steps. Includes survival skills, taking stock of the past, the tasks of the healing process, and guidelines for healing sexually.

Hunter, M. *Abused Boys: Healing for the Man Molested as a Child—The Neglected Victims of Sexual Abuse.* Lexington, Mass.: Heath, 1990.

Provides a complete account of the problems experienced by male survivors of childhood sexual abuse. This book is helpful to survivors, their partners, and helping professionals.

Divorce

Wallerstein, J. S., and Blakeslee, S. *Second Chances: Men, Women, and Children a Decade After Divorce.* New York: Ticknor & Fields, 1989.

Based on a longitudinal study. Provides a comprehensive account of the long-term emotional, economic, and psychological effects of divorce. The complexities of divorce are examined through actual experiences.

Dysfunctional Families

Forward, S. *Toxic Parents: Overcoming Their Hurtful Legacy and Reclaiming Your Life.* New York: Bantam Books, 1989.

Susan Forward describes the various types of toxic parents and illustrates, through case studies, how adults are affected by unhealthy parents. A section is devoted to describing a model of healing.

Gannon, J. P. *Soul Survivors: A New Beginning for Adults Abused as Children.* Englewood Cliffs, N.J.: Prentice-Hall, 1989.

Provides adults with help in determining whether they were abused as children and offers an understanding of abused families. Identifies problems experienced by adults from abusive families and proposes a healing process that includes the use of personal journals. Gannon also describes six adult survivors of abusive families.

Napier, N. J. *Recreating Your Self: Help for Adult Children of Dysfunctional Families.* New York: Norton, 1990.

This book offers a helpful resource for reclaiming the wounded child from the past and recreating a healthy self in the present. Examples are ·drawn from the author's life and clients' stories. Introspective exercises are included.

Emotional Abuse

Covitz, J. *The Family Curse: Emotional Child Abuse.* Boston: Sigo Press, 1986.

Provides descriptions of the full range of emotional child abuse, including examples drawn from case studies.

Elkind, D. *The Hurried Child: Growing Up Too Fast Too Soon.* Reading, Mass.: Addison-Wesley, 1988.

Identifies what parts of our society expect children to grow up too fast, and presents the crippling effects of hurrying children.

Holm, M. F. *Shall the Circle Be Unbroken?* Longmont, Colo.: Bookmaker's Guild, 1986.

Offers an in-depth study of the maltreatment of children and addresses the causes and patterns of abuse, as well as how children cope.

Spouse Abuse

Roy, M. *Children in the Crossfire: Violence in the Home—How Does It Affect Our Children?* Deerfield Beach, Fla.: Health Communications, 1988.

Explores issues related to spouse abuse and its impact on children. Innovative intervention strategies and remedial programs to prevent violence in future generations are presented.

Other Resources

Biffle, C. A. *Journey Through Your Childhood: A Write-In Guide for Reliving Your Past, Clarifying Your Present, and Charting Your Future.* Los Angeles: Jeremy P. Tarcher, 1989.

Offers memory-enhancing methods to recall and reconnect with childhood experiences. Can be described as a childhood scrapbook of lost memories to be used for healing.

Peele, S. *The Diseasing of America: Addiction Treatment Out of Control.* Lexington, Mass.: Heath, 1989.

Offers an in-depth analysis of the fallacies and futility of the alcohol-as-a-disease movement. Peel also suggest how to create a world worth living in.

White, J. L. *The Troubled Adolescent.* Elmsford, N.Y.: Pergamon Press, 1989.
    Explores such behaviors as depression, suicide, eating disorders, and drug abuse. Offers methods for coping with adolescent conflict, as well as models for diagnosis and treatment strategies.

Robert I. Witchel
Editor

References

Bass, E., and Davis, L. *The Courage to Heal: A Guide for Women Survivors of Child Sexual Abuse.* New York: Harper & Row, 1988.
Peele, S. *Diseasing of America: Addiction Treatment Out of Control.* Lexington, Mass.: Heath, 1989.

Robert I. Witchel is chair of the Department of Counselor Education at Indiana University of Pennsylvania. As a former counseling center director on two campuses, Dr. Witchel has worked extensively with high-risk college students from dysfunctional families. As a licensed psychologist, he has provided therapy to families experiencing difficulties with divorce and child custody, child abuse, incest, alcohol abuse, and other forms of family dysfunction.

INDEX

Ordering Information

New Directions for Student Services is a series of paperback books that offers guidelines and programs for aiding students in their total development—emotional, social, and physical, as well as intellectual. Books in the series are published quarterly in Fall, Winter, Spring, and Summer and are available for purchase by subscription as well as by single copy.

Subscriptions for 1991 cost $45.00 for individuals (a savings of 20 percent over single-copy prices) and $60.00 for institutions, agencies, and libraries. Please do not send institutional checks for personal subscriptions. Standing orders are accepted.

Single copies cost $13.95 when payment accompanies order. (California, New Jersey, New York, and Washington, D.C., residents please include appropriate sales tax.) Billed orders will be charged postage and handling.

Discounts for quantity orders are available. Please write to the address below for information.

All orders must include either the name of an individual or an official purchase order number. Please submit your order as follows:
    Subscriptions: specify series and year subscription is to begin
    Single copies: include individual title code (such as SS1)

Mail all orders to:
    Jossey-Bass Inc., Publishers
    350 Sansome Street
    San Francisco, California 94104

For sales outside of the United States contact:
    Maxwell Macmillan International Publishing Group
    866 Third Avenue
    New York, New York 10022

OTHER TITLES AVAILABLE IN THE
NEW DIRECTIONS FOR STUDENT SERVICES SERIES
Margaret J. Barr, Editor-in-Chief
M. Lee Upcraft, Associate Editor